# Confident Mum

Second Edition

## A Practical Guide
## to Managing Your Baby

Simone Boswell

Calm Baby Confident Mum:
A Practical Guide To Managing Your Baby

Copyright © 2007, 2008, 2011, 2012 Simone Boswell. (B Mus Ed)

First published August 2007
Revised and reprinted March 2008
Second Edition February 2011
Reprinted February 2012

National Library of Australia Cataloguing-in-Publication entry

　　Boswell, Simone.

　　Calm baby confident mum : a common sense guide to
　　managing your baby.

　　ISBN 978-0-9872605-2-9

　　Infants--Care.
　　Parenting.


Published by Boswell Bunch, Wollongong, Australia
http://www.boswellbunch.com
http://www.calmbabyconfidentmum.com


http://www.jaquesdesign.com

Printed in Australia

# Foreword

I have known Simone for more than ten years.

She is a loving wife, a capable mother of six, a home-schooler and a part-time music teacher. She regularly volunteers her time to speak to various community and church groups all over Wollongong and Sydney, and has also spoken in Canberra, Melbourne, Gold Coast, Adelaide and Perth. She is busy in her local church running groups for mums, and even occasionally finds time to read books and make her own cards!!

I have watched her raise her own six children with love and common sense. Each baby was calm, content and very bonnie. Although they each have their own unique personalities, all were very settled and established excellent sleep patterns very early in their life. Of course, each day is very full with six children in the home, but Simone and James have still managed to enjoy each other, their children, and reach out to generously help others in their parenting journey.

Most nights she answers email and phone questions from mums of babies all over the world. She speaks with wisdom in a straight-forward, no-nonsense manner, and has a very high success rate. Many mums will contact Simone for advice for their second and subsequent babies because what she advises works!

The principles outlined in this book will give you a calm baby. You will be a confident mum, having a basic framework for your day that covers almost all of the situations you will encounter in this precious first year. I followed these principles with my own precious blessings and experienced happy, settled, thriving babies.

I will be recommending this book to EVERY mum I know who is expecting a baby.

*Mel Hayde*
*HSIE and Special Ed teacher, Author TERRIFIC TODDLERS*

To my Lord and Saviour,
who gave me my babies,
and is the source of all wisdom.


To my wonderful husband,
best friend, and love,
James.


To my beautiful babies:
Madeline, Oliver, Rosemary,
Elliot, Jemima and Sebastian.


To my own precious mum,
Raema,
now singing with the angels.

# Table of Contents

# Introduction...

What an unforgettable sight our newborns are!

I always get a sense of shock after giving birth – wow, there really was a baby in there!

We spend so much time and energy focusing on prenatal classes to get us through labour, buying baby clothes and equipment, preparing our house and nursery, and reading magazines filled with happy smiling mothers and babies, that we can forget that there is a lot more to having a baby than all that.

The vast majority of mothers don't give much thought to what they will actually do with their baby when it comes home. Most mums think it will just work out without much preparation at all. But all the best labour advice, fancy clothes, flashy stroller, and colour co-ordinated nurseries in the world will not give you a settled, thriving baby. There is more to it.

When my husband and I were expecting our first baby, we spent time looking around at the people we knew who had babies. What did they do? What were their babies like? How did they cope? What advice did they have?

The vast majority of parents were tired and frazzled. Their babies cried a lot. They stopped coming to church, or going out much. They fussed over their babies excessively. They were full of 'just you wait' stories. While they were happy with their babies, it all seemed like a major disaster was looming!

On the other hand, we observed that some parents were calm and relaxed with their babies. Their babies were calm, relaxed and thriving, and all round it seemed like they were enjoying the experience.

*1*

We decided to ask *those* parents what they were doing that made them different from so many other families we had observed.

The common factor amongst so many of those calm and confident parents was the way they were managing their babies. We learned so much from them!

After many years of learning, and reading as widely as possible, I have become convinced that managing a baby on a flexible routine has been the most important factor in our babies being calm and settled.

The information I share on managing newborns, and older babies is based on all that I have learned from other parents, grandparents and books, and that which I put into practice in my own home.

I am not a medical practitioner, nurse, trained lactation consultant, or 'parenting expert'.

I am just a mum. Talking to other mums.

Therefore, this book should not replace medical advice in the case of illness or medical issues. Nor is it meant to explain every situation. This book is a *complementary* guide for frustrated and confused new mums, *not* a *comprehensive* guide on every situation that a new mum might encounter.

It is based on my experience of mothering six babies, talking with many hundreds of mothers about their babies, and reading widely. I have counselled many, many mums (and dads) via telephone and email, when speaking to community groups, and in person, for over ten years.

All mums are different. Some mums like everything lined up and perfectly organised down to the last second. Some mums are very unstructured and would rather go with the flow. Some mums are chaotic and stressed, other mums are calm and peaceful. My suggestions are not going to suit everyone! But when adapted and applied, they can suit a vast array of different mothers.

Every mother is free to decide exactly how she is going to feed and manage her own baby.

All babies are different, and I can't possibly cover all variables, but I do think that most babies can be managed in a similar way, and remain calm and settled. And I do think that a calm and settled baby gives confidence to mums. That what they are doing is contributing to that calm.

I believe that all babies are blessings from God, and that we should view them as a blessing to be enjoyed.

My passion is helping mums with their new babies – to encourage them, to support them and to inspire them. To help them to see how adding a baby to the family brings an enrichment that is hard to imagine before it happens. Our lives are just never the same again! My hope in putting my thoughts down on paper is that other mothers can learn how to enjoy their babies as I have, and in turn encourage and inspire other mums.

We live in a world saturated with choice, and most new parents are overwhelmed with all the available information on caring for babies – much of which is conflicting. Fads come and go, but my experience has been affected by the wisdom of older mothers and grandmothers, and has stood up against the baby management fashions that come and go.

In this book I have set things out in stages.

Very often mothers want to know what to do with their baby at a particular age. In dividing the information into age groups, I have allowed for new mums to turn quickly to each section that applies to them.

At the end of each age chapter, I have included some pages for reflection. Mums may like to reflect on how the baby is going, as well as how they are feeling about motherhood. It is always encouraging to look back and see how far we have come!

After those stages, I have included a few chapters on breastfeeding, crying, sleeping, and playtime. These sections will apply to all ages, but are best to read in the first few weeks and months.

I have followed up with a brief chapter for mums having their second babies, for mums with twins, premmies or special needs babies, and for new Dads.

And lastly a Final Word to mums, as they contemplate the coming years with a toddler.

My overall message in this book is one of helping mums and dads find a way to help them have a calm and settled baby through giving them a flexible routine, and in turn give them a confidence in their role as parents.

Thank you for taking the time to read my thoughts, and for sharing your own experiences with me. May God bless you on your parenting journey.

Simone.

*"Taste and see that the Lord is good.
Oh, the joys of those who take refuge in him!*

*Fear the Lord, you his godly people,
for those who fear him will have all they need.*

*Even strong young lions sometimes go hungry,*

*but those who trust in the Lord will lack no good thing."*
*Psalm 34:8-10*

*"Trust in the LORD with all your heart
and lean not on your own understanding;
in all your ways acknowledge him,
and he will make your paths straight."*

*Proverbs 3:5-6*

*"For I know the plans I have for you," declares the LORD, "plans to
prosper you and not to harm you, plans to give you hope and a future."*

*Jeremiah 29:11*

# Chapter One

# Newborns

Congratulations on the birth of your new baby, and welcome to Motherhood!

Now that this little baby has arrived in the world, it is up to you to make sure that he is (amongst other things) loved, cuddled and fed. Hopefully Dad will be ready and willing to offer support and encouragement to you and eager to offer plenty of love and cuddles for baby, but the feeding is most likely going to be your responsibility. Much of this first chapter will deal with getting feeding organised.

I do hope that as a new mother you are planning to breastfeed.

There is much evidence from the scientific community and anecdotally, that breastfeeding is the healthiest and most convenient way to feed a baby. It will take work though, and will not always be easy at first. But hang in there – it is worth it!

For some mothers breastfeeding will not be possible.

Perhaps there is a problem with the baby. Perhaps mum just can't establish a supply. Perhaps an injury makes it too difficult. Perhaps mum is required to take strong medication making breastfeeding difficult. Perhaps social or cultural factors make it difficult. Perhaps previous experiences make the prospect of breastfeeding too difficult.

Fortunately, whatever the reason behind such a decision we do live in an age where bottle-feeding is available and healthy. So your baby will still thrive if he ends up bottle-feeding earlier than you expected.

Most of the mechanical feeding tips I give here will refer to breastfeeding. However bottle-feeding babies will thrive on the same routines and management so there are still lots of helpful tips for those bottle-feeding mums.

A baby's day is going to fall into three main areas: **feedtime**, **awaketime**, and **sleeptime**.

Managing a newborn is about moving through these parts of the day in a way that leaves baby well fed, well rested and settled. The key to a settled baby (and mother) is getting these three areas flowing into each other in an order that works best for baby. In each section of this book we will discuss each of these three areas, and how they relate to a baby at different ages.

> A baby's day is going to fall into three main areas: **feedtime**, **awaketime**, and **sleeptime**.

So for a newborn, we will start with **feedtime.**

### Feedtime

Much of the first few days and weeks will focus on feeding your baby.

It is great if you can feed your baby soon after delivery (within an hour or two, or even sooner). If you have had a caesarian or a difficult delivery, or baby has a few problems that need to be seen to by the hospital staff, then breastfeeding may need to wait a little longer. But that's ok.

Your midwife will most likely show you how to feed that first time. However once you are settled into your room, you will have plenty of opportunities to try to figure it all out.

There is some more detailed information on positioning, latching on etc, in Chapter Nine - *Breastfeeding.*

For those first few days there are a few extra things to remember:

*The First Day:*

Some babies are really not very hungry in that first day and prefer to sleep. That's ok. Try to wake them every 3 hours or so for a feed, but don't panic if they are just not overly interested yet.

Sometimes a baby will sleep through that first day, and wake hungry and ready to go the next day. That's fine – a chance for you to rest and recover!

If baby is still not interested after a first day of being sleepy, then check with a doctor that he is not struggling with another issue.

**Always offer both breasts at a feeding session, if possible.**

Other babies are really hungry from the word go, and you may find yourself feeding them closer than 3 hours. That's ok too. These babies often stretch out their feeds on their own after a few days or weeks.

*The Next Few Days:*

Keep baby unwrapped to feed, as wrapping a newborn will encourage him to sleep.

Always offer both breasts at a feeding session if you can. You want your breasts to be stimulated as often as possible to encourage milk production. If baby regularly feeds for a long time on the first side, then you can detach him after 15-20 minutes or so and allow him to feed on the other side as well.

Feeding will generally take longer in the first week – your baby is learning to attach and suck. Be patient and enjoy lots of opportunities to sit and relax.

Try to keep feeds to around 45 minutes or less if possible. Otherwise you will soon be totally exhausted. After baby is finished feeding, wrap him up and allow him to sleep for a time so that he will have the energy to feed again next time.

If you have an alert baby, then you will spend more time with him awake and you'll likely find yourself working more on settling him. Sometimes babies are very efficient feeders from birth, allowing you more opportunities to see him with his eyes open!

A baby can drain a breast in only 5-7 minutes if he is suckling hard. Or these first few weeks may take up to 20 minutes to drain a breast. A baby that stays attached for much longer than that at each breast for each feeding will tire more easily and not suck strongly.

> **Try to give a complete feed every time rather than letting him 'sip and snooze'.**

After a feed, a baby should look full and content. Their eyes often roll back in their heads and they look a little 'drunk'!

Your basic aim in feeding after those first few days and then for the next few weeks, is to feed around 3 hourly. For example, this means that you might feed baby starting at around 7 o'clock, and then starting again around 10 o'clock - 3 hours later.

In between these feeds, baby should have a time of play (brief in these first few weeks), and a time of sleep before waking again for the next feed.

Some babies will get to 2½ hours and wake hungry and ready for a feed again. This is fine – feed your baby. Most babies stretch out to around 3 hours on their own after a few days or weeks.

Some babies insist on feeding continuously. This is more often because they like to 'suck and snooze' at the breast, rather than because they are so hungry they need to feed all the time. Try to give a complete feed every time rather than letting him 'sip and snooze'.

If baby is so sleepy that it takes an hour to wake him, then perhaps try waiting 3½-4 hours rather than 3 hours. He may then be more alert to feed. He might wake up a little more and decide to feed closer together in a few days. While it can be hard to wake a sleeping baby for a feed, this is important to do. It will help your baby fall into a routine more quickly, and will reduce the chance of your baby deciding to be alert through the night instead of the day.

It is usually a little unrealistic to plan all of your feed times in those first few weeks. That will come a little later. Hopefully you will soon settle into a fairly regular cycle of feeds. If you have a sleepy baby, then waking him regularly will help your routine to become consistent sooner. And it will help to keep your breasts stimulated which is going to help with your milk production.

A wise friend advised me to write down each time I fed the baby and to place it on the fridge during the day. This meant that when I was feeling be-fuddled I could have a look and see how my feeds were going and where I was up to.

What to do about nights? Most babies will continue to feed around the clock for a few weeks yet. Sometimes a mum might be concerned that she has a sleepy baby who needs to be woken every few hours, and so she might set an alarm so that she can keep feeding regularly. It is best not to let them sleep longer than 5 hours or so in those first few weeks, to give your milk time to establish.

*When Your Milk Comes In:*

Before your milk comes in, your breasts may not feel like they have milk inside. But they do! Hormones are wonderful for milk production and they will cause your breasts to fill with rich milk in a few days. For some mothers it happens in just a day or two, for other mothers it can take up to five or six days. But don't despair those first few days – your baby is getting everything he needs from the rich colostrum.

Once your milk does come in, you may struggle with engorgement. This can be rather painful and you may find cool washers placed on the breast give some relief. It can also make attachment difficult. Hand expressing some milk before you try to attach baby will soften the nipple area and help him attach better. This will normally settle down in a day or two and become a lot more comfortable.

After a feed and once your milk has 'come in', your breasts should feel drained or less full.

## Awaketime

The next activity in baby's day, after **feedtime,** is **awaketime.**

> It is important that feeding time comes at the *start* of awaketime, not at the end.

After he has had his feed, he will have a short time of being awake until he is tired and ready for a sleep. This awaketime is the total time that baby is 'up' – i.e. fed, burped, changed, cuddled. And it is important that feeding time comes at the *start* of awaketime, not at the end.

Your newborn will probably not spend much time awake in the first week. Some are even very sleepy for the first three or four weeks. Others are more alert from the beginning.

After a feed place him on the bed, chair or floor. Unwrap him and allow him to quietly look around. By placing him flat on his back like this, you are allowing him to stretch out his legs a little. This helps to keep him awake if he is sleepy and allows him to kick a little extra air out.

Try not to excessively stimulate him too much during these early days – it will only tire him more easily, and he may struggle to sleep and feed properly. Even noise like TV or radio can be over-stimulating for some newborns.

He should lie quietly for a few minutes during which you can enjoy him. Once he has been awake for around 45 minutes since the start of his feed, he will probably start to tire and be ready for a sleep.

After a few weeks he will be much more responsive during his awaketime, so be patient.

## Sleeptime

Once he has had some time awake (or once he has finished his long feed if he is a slow, sleepy feeder) then it is time for bed again. These newborns are so tiny- they really do need lots of sleep.

> **These newborns are so tiny, they really do need lots of sleep.**

Wrap him up nice and tight. This will help him to feel cozy and secure, and will help stop him from startling himself. Unwrapped newborns so often struggle to get to sleep. Wrap him as tightly as you can, with his little arms bent up around his shoulders (midwives are good at this). He should look like a cosy, squashed caterpillar. If you try to wrap him with his arms down, you might find that he squirms out of his wrap.

Place him in his bed and allow him to fuss for a minute or two if he needs to.

If he continues to remain unsettled, you can try to soothe him by cuddling or rubbing his back for a few minutes or until he stops fussing. If he is very distressed after 5 minutes or so, give him a soothing cuddle and try again once he has calmed down.

Do try to avoid picking him up and putting him back down over and over these first few days and weeks. It is quite stimulating and probably won't really help him get to sleep.

Try to avoid always allowing your baby to fall asleep in your arms. It doesn't do any harm from time to time, but if they learn that that is the only way to get to sleep, it can be difficult to break the habit down the track.

Another wise friend advised me to try to put them to bed awake, if possible. This allows them to learn to fall asleep by themselves. My newborns have usually been rather sleepy, so it hasn't always been possible during those first days. It was a handy bit of advice to remember, especially for later when they became more alert.

More tips for sleeping and a suggested routine can be found in Chapter Eleven - *Sleeping*.

**Extra Bits…**

**Nursery.** I have always preferred my babies to sleep in another room to me during the night. While some of them have slept in my room, I have found that I sleep better if I can't hear them snuffling next to me! Babies are quite noisy when they sleep, and a new mother is so finely tuned into them. She can be constantly woken up each time her baby makes a noise.

> Try to put them to bed awake, if possible. This helps them to learn to fall asleep by themselves.

Some mothers have their babies in with them because they prefer it, or they have a small house, other children, sickness, or whatever. That of course is fine – he is your baby! My last baby Sebastian spent more nights in our room because of lack of space. He was rather noisy in his sleep though, and I think we both slept better when he was just a little further away! Sometimes hearing every snuffly noise is not a help to a tired mum.

Baby monitors are popular, but were unnecessary in my house. My babies make a loud noise when they want to be heard! But some people find a monitor helpful if they have a big house, like to work in the garden, or just feel more at ease being able to hear baby while he is sleeping.

**Dummies**. Mothers often ask me about dummies (pacifiers).

It is really a personal decision for the parents. Some parents start out deciding they don't want one. Some of those change their minds. Other parents start out planning to use one, but then find their baby refuses.

I have chosen to use a dummy in those first few weeks with all mine. We found that our babies really like to keep sucking after a feed, even though they are not hungry. Using a dummy has been very soothing for them, and they have settled quickly after taking it. Some babies like mine also have problems positioning their tongues when they feed, and dummies can help them have some practice sucking with their tongues down.

I learned to restrict that dummy to bedtime rather than awaketime, as they sometimes became so dependent on it that they loudly complained when it was taken away for a photo! My first little baby Madeline was rather attached to her dummy and made rather a loud noise whenever it was removed! I learned that after a few months it was probably a good idea to wean them off it.

> **My babies have always been very relaxed after a bath. They tend to feed well, then sleep well.**

Some parents are concerned that if they start using a dummy with their babies it will lead to enslavement – a baby who isn't happy unless they have their dummy in. Or a baby who needs their dummy put back multiple times through the night. Or a three year old who still wanders around with a dummy. The choice is very much that of the parents so you can feel free to do as you wish.

**Bathing**. After arriving home from hospital, we have always bathed before the last night feed, usually around 11pm. This has been a time that my husband can spend with the baby before bringing him to me for a last feed for the night. My babies have always been very relaxed after a bath. They tend to feed well, then sleep well.

Some parents prefer to bath baby during the morning as is the routine in hospital. I found this a busy time, especially with several little 'helpers' in tow. However, bathing baby time is whatever works best for each family.

**Nappy changing**. I learned over the years that using commercial baby wipes was irritating my baby's skin. My little baby Oliver had particularly bad nappy rash. So instead I used wash cloths dampened with warm water. These could then be tossed into a nappy bucket, along with cloth nappies (when I was using them). I then washed them through the machine each night, and hung them on the line to dry in the morning.

> **Hopefully, baby will settle into a fairly predictable routine of around 3 hours or so between feeds.**

It was more convenient to use baby wipes when I was out and about. A damp cloth in a plastic bag is also rather simple if your baby is struggling with commercial wipes causing nappy rash or eczema.

I also discovered that it was quite convenient to change my baby's nappies on the washing machine rather than a bulky change table. The taps, tub and nappy bucket are right next to the washing machine, so it was all very simple and helpful in a small house.

**Dirty Nappies**. How often should they have dirty nappies? Plenty of wet and dirty nappies are usually a good sign – good input gives good output. Wet nappies particularly are an important indicator of baby getting enough milk. However infrequent dirty nappies (especially with breastfed babies) do not necessarily mean there is a problem. When my first child Madeline routinely went ten days between dirty nappies, I questioned my GP, only to be assured that his babies did the same and it was ok. Some of mine have had long stretches between dirty nappies. Others like my Oliver went five (or more) times every day!

If your baby suddenly has long periods between dirty nappies, or hard stools, it is probably worth checking with your doctor.

> **Remember to look after yourself too!**

If all else is going well (weight gain good, plenty of wet nappies, settled baby), then it is probably quite ok to have a week or so between dirty nappies in those first few months. Just make sure you travel with plenty of supplies in case that drought breaks...

## The Next Few Weeks...

The next few weeks will see your baby growing and changing so much.

You will start to feel much more like your old self and will enjoy moving around with much more ease after your big belly! If you have had a caesarian or difficult delivery, it will take a few weeks to feel normal. But it will happen in time.

Hopefully baby will settle into a fairly predictable routine of around 3 hours or so between feeds. Awaketimes will remain at around the 45 minute mark (from the start of the feed until sleeptime).

Your milk supply should establish and stabilise. Hopefully breastfeeding will become a much more enjoyable experience.

Remember to look after yourself too.

Eat well. This is not the time to diet in order to squeeze back into your jeans. You won't be able to make healthy milk and keep yourself healthy as well, if you are not eating well.

Drink, drink, drink. Lots of water is needed to prevent dehydration.

Slow down. Take it easy these first few weeks and allow your body to have time to recover. Even if you feel well, you will cope much better if you are resting rather than running around.

Rest. Always try to have a snooze during the day to give you the energy to keep going through the night. You are now on call 24/7 so you will need to rest when you can. Your housework can wait!

## Frequently Asked Questions...

**My baby is 3 weeks old, but he was 4 weeks early. I am having trouble keeping him up for an hour of awaketime – he just keeps falling asleep. Am I doing something wrong?**

Many newborns are very sleepy and have few moments of awaketime in a day. Babies born even just a few weeks early have even more trouble staying awake!

For now your baby will probably just feed and sleep, with perhaps one or two times in the day where he might stay awake for a short time after a feed. But that's ok, because in another few weeks, you will probably find he wakes up much more and is able to have some 'playtime' with you.

Just remember too that premmie babies really don't cope well with too much stimulation – it tires them out and they tend to 'shut down'. Feeding is very important for them to grow and gain weight, and this is where they need to put their energy. If we keep these little ones up for too long or use up their energy 'playing', they will be too tired to eat properly and not gain weight so well.

Patience! More tips for premmies can be found in Chapter Fourteen.

**My baby is 2 weeks old. He seems to be awake a lot! He isn't settling well, and cries much of the day. What can I do?**

There are several things to consider here.

Is your baby hungry? How is your attachment? Are you sure your baby is getting full feeds? If you are struggling with attachment then it can be helpful to visit a Lactation Consultant who can observe you feeding and see if there needs to be an adjustment made.

If you are ok with your attachment then consider if your baby may need more feeds in his day.

Perhaps your baby doesn't seem hungry. He isn't interested in added feeds, he is gaining weight quickly and has plenty of wet and dirty nappies. It may then help to look at his routine and sleeps.

If baby is over stimulated during his awaketime, he will often struggle to 'wind down' to sleep. And if he isn't sleeping well, he will struggle to feed well.

Check that the time that he is 'up' – ie, fed, burped, changed, cuddled – is not too long. 45 minutes or so is plenty for a newborn. Wrap him tightly and spend a few minutes cuddling him gently to give him time to relax ready for sleep before putting him down.

This does not mean cuddling him to sleep every time!

He will do better in the long term if he can fall asleep on his own. Once he is calm, pop him into bed and give him possibly 5 -10 minutes of fussing before picking him up to soothe and start again.

Try to avoid pacing the hallway through the night or day with him – this is over stimulating and doesn't usually result in much beyond a tired mummy (or dad). He is better to fuss for a few minutes in his bed so that he can have a go at self-settling.

Patience – he will get there!

## My baby is 4 weeks old. He seems to have his days and nights mixed up!

If your baby is happy to slumber all day but party all night, then it is time to help him change things around.

It will help enormously to consistently wake baby for regular 3 hourly feeds through the day and pop him back to bed at that 45 minute (or so) mark. Resist the urge to let him sleep for irregular times through the day, or for as long as he wishes way past that 3 hour mark. Better a few days of unsettledness to get back on track, than more nights of crying and struggling to get him to sleep.

It is also wise to make sure that your night feeds happen in an atmosphere of quiet and dim light. Stimulation should be kept to a minimum. Even TV can be too much for a newborn in the night. Just keep a big difference between day and night feeds!

## Grandma spent the day here yesterday, and now my 3 week old is completely out of whack. How do I get him back on track again?

It is funny how they can be as good as gold for Grandma but then fall apart the next day! All quite normal and to be expected. When you have a big day with visitors, or you have been out and about, expect a difficult day to follow. Stick to your normal routine as much as you can. Be a little flexible if you need to be. But not too flexible – things take longer to settle when we abandon our routines totally.

## My 3 week old baby seems quite settled – sleeping and such, but she is just not gaining any weight. I am feeding 3 hourly – what more can I do?

Firstly, don't panic.

Next, have a clinic sister or lactation specialist check that your attachment is going ok. A poor attachment can lead to inefficient sucking and slow weight gain.

Make sure you are waking baby approximately 3 hourly around the clock for a feed. Give her 10-15 minutes each side, broken up into 5 minute intervals if she is very sleepy. Use a hand held breast pump after three feeds each day, and store any milk collected into a bottle to be given to her after the next feed (or after the last feed of the day, if you like). Expressing milk in this way should help to increase your milk supply.

Make sure that you are eating and drinking really well. Some mums are used to eating bird-like meals, and you just won't be able to sustain a good supply unless you eat more. Drink *Sustagen*, or another supplement to boost your supply.

If baby is settled and sleeping, then continue on this course until she is 6 weeks old. Check in with your clinic or doctor each week (or more often if they suggest) to check progress. Hopefully your milk supply should be more established once you get to 6 weeks. This can be a turning point for many mums. The slow weight-gain baby often starts to gain, and things usually start to settle down.

If you find that baby is becoming increasingly unsettled-waking hungry, fussing at the feeds, or not gaining weight at that 6 week mark, it may be time to supplement your feeding with a bottle of formula (perhaps in the evening). Sometimes just one or two bottles a day can maintain baby's weight, along with breastfeeding the rest of the day.

Sometimes the introduction of a bottle means that breastfeeding may just not be possible long term this time around. If you have tried everything and you have had support from your clinic or doctor, and baby is still not gaining weight, then over to bottles it may be. This is quite disappointing for many mums, but please don't despair. Your baby will still be fine on a bottle. And there is still the possibility that you will be able to breastfeed your next baby.

**My 5 week old baby is quite settled and feeding well. I have noticed however, that when I put her to bed, she just lies there for half an hour or so before falling asleep. Should I keep her up longer?**

No. Your baby is spending this quiet time in her bed just resting and preparing for sleep. She is winding down, relaxing and enjoying her space. Keeping her up longer at each awaketime now will most likely only over-stimulate her so that she will actually struggle more to get to sleep. She will cope better with a longer awaketime when she is a little older.

**My sister bought me a sling to carry my new baby in. Should I let him sleep in it during the day?**

Some mothers choose to sling their babies through the day, which is their choice to make. It seems rather cosy and 'natural' but can have its drawbacks too.

Babies who are kept in slings all day will often sleep and feed erratically. Over time they may learn to need that sling in order to get to sleep, which can make night times a struggle. Long-term use may lead to back problems for some mothers.

If you are looking to have a flexible routine for your day rather than unpredictable feeds and sleeps, you may be better to limit your sling to outings rather than allowing baby to depend on it for all of his sleeps. I had times of using my slings shopping, at church and even the cricket one day with Sebastian! Some slings are definitely more comfortable than others, so choose that sling wisely.

**My baby is 3 weeks old. My nipples are very sore, cracked and blistering from the feeds. I have tried putting breast milk on them, Lansinoh cream, airing them to dry, different feeding positions, breast shields and expressing milk. But nothing is helping and I feel like giving up.**

These sore nipples are a big problem - I KNOW! You have tried all you can, and I did find that Lansinoh was definitely the best thing that worked for me. I did also use shields - a good idea to give those nipples a little rest.

But ultimately, they do need to 'toughen up', and this only happens when you are not using the shields. Perhaps you could try one side at a time? Speak to a Lactation Consultant too to see if there is anything in your attachment which can be adjusted.

If you can hang in there until the 6 week mark, you should begin to see some noticeable improvement.

# Newborn Baby Review
*After 2 weeks reflect on how baby is going...*

## Weight and Growth
Weight:
Length:
Nappies are:

## Feedtime
Attachment:      good ☐ sometimes OK ☐ still getting there ☐

Duration:               Comfort:

    20 mins or under ☐    mostly comfortable ☐ becoming

    20-40 mins ☐          more comfortable ☐

    40-60 mins ☐         still uncomfortable ☐

Baby is usually feeding around

               every 2 hrs or less ☐  2-3 hrs ☐  3+ hrs ☐

Any clicking noises while feeding? nipples sore? any concerns?

Other reflections on feeding...

*if bottle feeding* mls per feed:

## Sleeptime
Baby is going to bed:               awake ☐  asleep ☐

Duration of baby's sleep:
    less than 60 mins ☐  60-90 mins ☐  90-120 mins ☐  120+ mins ☐

Resettling:         most sleeps ☐  some sleeps ☐  rarely ☐

Other reflections on sleeping...

## Awaketime
during awaketime my baby...

## Mum Reflections

The best things about these 2 weeks have been...

The hardest things about these 2 weeks have been...

I am thankful to God for...

After 2 weeks I am feeling...

*Mothers have a special way of filling homes with love, and when the home is filled with love you'll always find God spoken of there.*
*Helen Steiner Rice*

*Now like infants at the breast, drink deep of God's pure kindness.*
*1 Peter 2:2*

Chapter Two                          Six week olds

What bright-eyed little things our babies are at 6 weeks!

By this time they are looking around the room, watching our faces intently, starting to smile. Some are even cooing. Some will be able to focus on a toy or mobile for a short time. Their faces are starting to round out nicely, and they love to flap their little arms and legs.

If you are breastfeeding, you will hopefully be feeling much better about it all now. Those first few weeks can be tiring, painful and hard work. Around 6 weeks many mums feel much more comfortable when they feed, and their milk supply is starting to feel like it's settled into a nice pattern. Some mums may have had difficult birth experiences – perhaps a caesarian, or lots of stitches. By 6 weeks, you should be feeling close to physically normal again.

Hopefully your baby is also feeling much more settled. If you are planning to continue feeding on a flexible routine, let's have a look at what can be expected around now...

Here is a sample routine, based on a 3 hour routine:

|  |  |
|---|---|
| 6:00 | feed (breast/bottle), then awaketime |
| 6:45 | sleep |
| 9:00 | feed, then awaketime |
| 9:45 | sleep |
| 12:00 | feed, then awaketime |
| 12:45 | sleep |
| 3:00 | feed, then awaketime |
| 3:45 | sleep |
| 6:00 | feed, then awaketime |
| 6:45 | sleep |
| 9:00 | bath, feed |
| 9:30 | sleep |
| 11:30 | feed, then straight back to bed – no awaketime |
| ? | Middle-of-the-night feed(s) |

Of course, all times are approximate and you can start your day anytime you wish. Just change the times to make it work for you and your baby.

## Feedtime

*Night Feeds*

You probably won't need to wake baby for his middle-of-the-night feed. Some mums who are concerned with their milk supply may continue to set their alarms to feed their babies in the middle of the night, in case their baby doesn't wake on his own. But for most mums, any other night feeds will happen whenever baby is hungry.

Around 6 weeks some babies may be starting to stretch their night feeds. These stretches will gradually get further and further apart.

This might look like feeds at around 11.30pm, 3.30, then 6.00am. But a few nights later: 11.30, 4.30, 7.00am. And so on, until they are really skipping a feed.

> **Babies are getting bigger and feeding more efficiently.**

Sometimes a baby will just suddenly skip a middle-of-the-night feed. This is always a surprise for mum, but if baby is happy then it shouldn't be a problem. My little Madeline did this – it gave me a shock but she was quite fine.

When a baby does eventually drop a night feed, some mums worry that they may not have given their babies enough feeds across the whole day. But their babies are getting bigger and feeding more efficiently. They no longer need that middle-of-the-night feed to get them through.

*Morning Wake-up Calls...*

Six weeks is a time for some mums to start wondering if their babies should be starting each day at around the same time. Occasionally a consistent morning wake-up time will happen earlier than 6 weeks. Other babies start at the same time around now, and others will wait for a few more weeks.

If your baby is still asleep at the time you wish to start your day, you may need to wake him up in order to keep on track. For some families that morning start time might be 6am, others 7am, and others later. It doesn't really matter as long as it works for your family.

Perhaps you will compromise with your baby, who may stubbornly continue to wake around 6am, when you had hoped for a 7am start. A little compromise is part of life with a baby!

What do you do if baby wakes for a feed at say 4.30am, but you are aiming to start the day at around 6am?

Basically you have three main choices:

1. Feed at 4.30am, and then wake baby for another feed at 6am.

2. Feed at 4.30am, then feed around 3 hours later (7.30am), and continue a 3 hourly pattern from then on.

3. Feed at 4.30am, then wake for a feed at around 6.30am, and then gradually adjust feeds a little each time until you are back on track sometime during the day.

*Flexible Feed Times*

Of course all feed times are able to be a little flexible. If your baby wakes a little early and is hungry and wanting a feed, then go ahead and feed him.

**There is no need to listen to a hungry baby cry!**

Similarly, if you have been out and your baby has had a long awaketime and needs a little more sleep, then you should let him sleep a little longer.

It does help to generally have about the same gap between feeds as often as possible. This will mean waking your baby for a feed if he hasn't woken on his own.

> **Of course all feed times are able to be a little flexible.**

Sometimes a sleepy baby will need to be woken almost every feed.

If baby is sleeping well, gaining weight, and you are sure that your milk supply is plentiful then you could consider moving to a 3½ hourly routine. This will mean dropping a feed. But if all is going well it shouldn't be a problem. As our babies get bigger and stronger they feed much more efficiently, so you often don't need to feed them quite so frequently.

Anytime a baby of this age starts waking early on a regular basis and shows signs of being hungry, then simply go back to feeding as often as he needs it.

4 hourly feeds (rather than 3) will work ok for a few babies, especially bottle fed babies. As long as baby is not hungry and is gaining weight etc, then this is fine. It is definitely much too early to go longer than 4 hours between day feeds on a regular basis.

> **Generally have about the same gap between feeds as often as possible.**

*Keeping Records*

It is always helpful to check your growth charts (obtained from baby clinics, doctor, Blue Book or hospital). You could also keep a record of wet and dirty nappies as well as number and length of feeds, and weight/height gains. Or you could have baby weighed every few weeks at the clinic or chemist. This will encourage you in what you are doing to feed and care for your baby. A six to eight week check is common at this age anyway, which is an ideal time to make sure baby is growing normally.

*Feeding Concerns*

Please use this opportunity to discuss any concerns with your baby health nurse or doctor.

If you are breastfeeding then it is important that you attempt to feed on both sides at each feed. If you don't do this you are risking a lack of stimulation on one side for a period of possibly 6 hours or more. This is not good for maintaining milk supply!

If your baby feeds for a long time on the first side and won't feed on the second side, then it can help if you keep track of the time and detach him halfway. If for example he feeds 20 minutes on that first side (and then none on the second), simply detach him (*gently*) after 10 minutes. Give him a burp and pop him on the other side to finish.

Always swap starting-sides at each feed to balance the strongest sucking. If you are having trouble remembering which side you are up to, you can keep track by writing it on the fridge or swapping a nappy pin from bra-strap to strap each feed.

If your baby has been characterised by spending longer than 30 minutes feeding then it may also be time to restrict the feeding time. Very slow feeders can end up with reduced playtime. They also tend to fall asleep feeding. Baby can become more awake when he is supposed to be sleeping. Most babies do not actually feed for that whole time anyway. Instead they are usually 'sipping, snacking and snoozing'. 20 - 30 minutes of feeding is plenty for most 6 week olds.

> **20 - 30 minutes of feeding is plenty for most 6 week olds.**

Sometimes a baby is particularly efficient and mum worries that they don't spend enough time feeding. If your baby pulls himself off after a few minutes and doesn't want any more, then that's fine. You have a strong sucker! You can't force your baby to drink if he really doesn't want to. As long as he is growing, happy and sleeping well, then all is fine.

Sometimes mum's let-down is so strong that baby can't drink fast enough. If your let-down comes in strong and fast then it is helpful to pull baby off the breast as soon as the let-down begins. Allow the milk to fall onto a cloth nappy or towel until the flow subsides. Then pop baby back on again to continue the feed. This will help the baby to avoid swallowing too much air which can lead to a tummy ache.

Sometimes families need to do things slightly differently with their schedules to take into consideration a shift-working father or a mum who prefers to go to bed early and feed at 2am or another unusual situation. This is all fine – do what suits your family.

## Awaketime

*Kicking Around*

After feeding and burping I suggest giving baby a short time on the floor to kick his arms and legs.

> **Watch out that you don't over-stimulate your six week old baby.**

Rocker chairs are great but they do tend to squash up those little bodies. Which doesn't help if they have some trapped air that needs to come out! A short kick time on the floor is handy to give that trapped air an opportunity to escape. Then they can snuggle up in their cosy rocker chair or in someone's lap for a little while!

Other awaketime activities include playing with their arms and legs, 'talking' with them and giving them some space to watch the activity around the room. Some babies might focus on a mobile for a short time.

*Over-stimulation*

Watch out that you don't over-stimulate your six week old baby.

I have had mothers tell me they spend this time dancing around the room, in order for their babies to be well stimulated so they'll do better at school! This is *not* the time for these vigorous activities! That will come a little later.

For now your baby needs a fairly peaceful time awake, or he will really struggle to wind down for a sleep.

Awaketime for a six week old baby on a three hourly routine should be around 45 minutes. This time includes feeding, changing and playtime.

While it seems like such a short time, your baby is still so little at this age. He will get a longer playtime when he is bigger and can cope better. It is preferable to have a shorter playtime and settled baby, than a long playtime and a baby who is unsettled through the night because he is too over-tired to sleep.

If your baby is on a four hourly routine, then 60 minutes should be plenty of time. Any more, and he will struggle to resettle during naps.

More on awaketime activities in Chapter Twelve.

## Sleeptime

### Getting to Sleep

Once it is time for bed, wrap your baby up nice and tight, give him a yummy cuddle and kiss, and pop him into bed.

Some babies are happy to go off to sleep with a dummy at this age, and this is fine. My little Rosie was like this.

Some babies will have a little cry as they go down but then quickly resettle themselves, and this is also fine. My little Sebastian was like this.

Some babies will go down happily, remain quiet for a short while, and then have a little cry, and this too is fine. Just like my little Oliver.

Sometimes babies just need to have a good cry to get the rest of their excess energy out. They often wiggle and squirm much like you or I do, as they get comfortable for a sleep. My Elliot!

If your baby has been crying gustily for 5-10 minutes or more, then you should go in and pick him up, give him a soothing cuddle until he is settled again, and then try again to put him back down. Try not to unsettle him by unnecessarily changing his nappy or unwrapping him. Give him another 10 minutes or so before trying to resettle him again.

The more often you go in and out and in and out and pick him up and put him down... the more unsettled he might become.

That is why I wait for 10 minutes or so- to give him time to settle himself.

## *Staying Asleep*

If he wakes part-way into his sleep (often at around that 45 minute mark), give him a few minutes to see if he will resettle himself. If he is still crying gustily after 5 or 10 minutes or so, then go in and pick him up and soothe him.

> **If he wakes part-way into his sleep, give him a minute or two to see if he will resettle himself.**

If he persists in crying even once you have picked him up, then consider that it might be getting close to the next feedtime, and so he may be hungry. If so- of course you will feed him!

If he is happy once he is picked up and doesn't seem hungry, then you can try putting him down again for 10 minutes or so to see if he will resettle again.

## *Fussy Time*

It is not uncommon for babies to have a regular period of unsettledness each day. This is often called the '**fussy time**' and tends to occur during the late afternoon/evening. It can also come in the morning, or early afternoon.

If this fussy time is becoming normal for your baby then you will need to find a technique that works best for your family. Sometimes getting them up and sitting them happily in their rocker chair for 10-15 minutes or so is enough to get them back into sleep mode. Sometimes an extra feed now and again can help (especially if they are hungry because mum's supply has dipped a little). Usually though, calm resettling is the most effective.

If it happens at the same time each day then you can be prepared rather than disappointed.

More tips for sleeping can be found in Chapter Eleven.

### The Next Six Weeks...

Where are you going with your baby's routine during the next six weeks?

If you are feeding around 3 hourly now, then you may consider moving to feeding closer to 3½ hourly some time in the next 6 weeks. Some babies will even go up to 4 hours between most feeds by around 12-14 weeks.

This is dependent on your milk supply keeping up. Most mums don't have any difficulties with their supply but some do. Be mindful that you drink lots of water, eat really well and rest when you can.

> **Be mindful that you drink lots of water, eat really well and rest when you can.**

If baby needs to feed at around 3 hours for longer, then that's also fine.

By the time your baby reaches 3 months, you can extend his awaketime to 1 hour. He will be much more alert for longer by then.

### Other Bits...

If your baby is crying for prolonged periods, for no apparent reason and you are feeding on a flexible schedule, then check that your milk supply is ok (more tips on that in Chapter Nine), and go and see your doctor. Very occasionally some babies have allergies and such that are best discovered earlier rather than later.

Another possibility could be a pain in the tummy caused by wind or gulping milk. Maybe you need to let your milk flow onto a towel to reduce the flow after a powerful let down. Rubbing his tummy or back may help. You can even try an over-the-counter medication, to see if that helps things settle down. Check with your doctor before giving your baby medication.

A baby who cries for prolonged periods has often just found himself in a cycle of over-tiredness that takes a few days of consistent routine feeds and limited awaketimes before starting to settle. We will look more into that in the next chapter.

## Frequently Asked Questions...

**My 6 week old is still so sleepy, I can't keep him awake after a feed. But then he wakes up during his nap and won't settle!**

It is so very important to keep them awake during and after feeds. If you have tried a wet washer on his arms, legs and face, undressing him, and tickling his face, then perhaps placing him flat on the floor partly undressed might help. Some of them like to snuggle while being cuddled which just keeps sending them back to sleep. If they are flat on the floor, they are much more likely to wake up. This is why they often wake up for nappy changes.

If he has been in the habit of snoozing after feeds and waking during naps, it will take a few days of work to get him back on track. But stick with it! Once he is staying awake for his 45 or so minutes of total awaketime and sleeping until the next feed, it will be worth the effort!

**My 6 week old is so wide awake! He doesn't like going to sleep at all, and is quite happy watching all the activity. He is very unsettled through the night, though.**

Teaching a baby to sleep during the day is very important if you want him to sleep at night. When babies don't get enough sleep they become 'wired' and can't wind down to a regular sleep pattern. If they *don't* learn to move through the sleep phases of deep and active sleep during the day, they will struggle to sleep well at night. Both adults and babies move through these sleep cycles during sleep and now is a good time to help your baby manage those cycles of sleep. More on sleep cycles in Chapter Eleven.

Persist with popping him to bed after a short awaketime ,and resettling until he learns to self-settle. This will pay off as he gets bigger.

## When is it best to take my 6 week old out – during his awaketime, or his sleeptime?

I suggest going out straight after a feed. He may have some wake time while you are out, and then fall asleep in the pram. He may also be quite wakeful and not have a good sleep while out. That is fine. Just pop him back to bed when you return. He may be a little unsettled going back to bed – that would be because he is a little over-stimulated, but that's fine. Some patient resettling will help him go back to sleep. You may need to have a shorter awaketime next cycle to make up for him being wakeful while he was out.

## My baby is waking at different times in the night. Sometimes 3am, sometimes 4am, sometimes later. How do I start the day at the same time when the nights are all over the place?

At 6 weeks you may not start the day at exactly the same time. This time of stretching night sleep and then waking at different times to feed is rather short lived. It seems long now but will soon be over. If you are feeding on a 3 hour routine then you will mostly just wake up baby 3 hours after his previous night feed for that first morning feed of the day. If you prefer to let him sleep a little longer (and he is happy to) so you can start at a more convenient time, then feel free. Just go 3 hourly from then. Likewise if that first gap is shorter than 3 hours, that's fine too.

## Sometimes my baby's dirty nappies are green! Is this ok?

I do remember the first time I saw a green nappy! After that mustard colour it is a shock. It is probably nothing to worry about though. If you are breastfeeding, his nappies may be affected by your own diet. Some people believe that Green nappies are related to baby gulping air while feeding. I haven't noticed that the colour of dirty nappies has affected my babies much at all.

Of course if those unusual nappies are accompanied by unusual behaviour, then go check with your doctor.

## My baby is due to have his needles tomorrow. Should I be worried that he'll be traumatised?

It is far more common for mum to be traumatised by baby's first needles than baby!

While there is some evidence that a small number of babies have reactions from needles, these babies are by far the minority.

Unfortunately, your sleepy 8 week old will get a rude shock when that needle goes in, and his won't be the only tears flowing. His pain is very short lived however, so try not to worry. You can check with your doctor about giving him baby paracetamol which may help cushion the pain a little.

Sometimes a baby may be a little unsettled for a day or two after vaccinations,. Give him an extra cuddle or feed, and he will probably be himself again by the next day. Again, if you are at all concerned with his behaviour after his needles, check with the doctor.

**My 7 week old slept through the night two nights ago, but last night woke for a feed again. Will he ever sleep through again?**

Congratulations on that first night of sleep!

It is quite normal for a baby to stop and start his sleeping through at this age. Think of it as two steps forward one step back. Once he sleeps through for three or four nights in a row, you can be quite confident that he is well on the way to sleeping through regularly. In the meantime, patience – he will get there ☺.

# Six Week Baby Review
*After 6 weeks reflect on how baby is going...*

## Weight and Growth
Weight:
Length:
Nappies are:

## Feedtime
Attachment:          good ☐  sometimes OK ☐  still getting there ☐

Duration:                              Comfort:
            20 mins or under ☐            mostly comfortable ☐  becoming
                    20-40 mins ☐                    more comfortable ☐
                    40-60 mins ☐                  still uncomfortable ☐

Baby is usually feeding around
                        every 2 hrs or less ☐  2-3 hrs ☐  3+ hrs ☐

Any clicking noises while feeding? nipples sore? any concerns?

Other reflections on feeding...

*if bottle feeding* mls per feed:

## Sleeptime
Baby is going to bed:                        awake ☐  asleep ☐

Duration of baby's sleep:
    less than 60 mins ☐   60-90 mins ☐   90-120 mins ☐   120+ mins ☐

Resettling:                  most sleeps ☐  some sleeps ☐  rarely ☐

Other reflections on sleeping...

## Awaketime
during awaketime my baby...

**Mum reflections**

The best things about these 6 weeks have been...

The hardest things about these 6 weeks have been...

I am thankful to God for...

After 6 weeks I am feeling...

*Lord, when my soul is weary and my heart is tired sore,*
*And I have that failing feeling, that I can't take any more;*
*then let me know the refreshing found in simple, childlike prayer,*
*When the kneeling soul knows surely that a listening Lord is there.*
*Ruth Bell Graham*
*from "Sitting By My Laughing Fire"*

*Give thanks to the Lord for He is good!*
*His faithful love endures forever.*
*Psalm 136:1*

# Three month olds

What gorgeous babies we have at 3 months!

They are filling out more and starting to giggle and coo. They have such bright and alert eyes as they start to really take in all their surroundings. Some are grasping toys or batting mobiles. Their heads are much more steady and some can bounce with their legs.

This is also a time of change as those babies on a flexible routine start to stretch their feeds and their awaketimes, and move right out of their newborn phase toward their very alert stage (which usually starts at around 4 months).

So what might their routines look like at 3 months?

Some babies have moved onto around 4 hours between feeds at 3 months, some are still on 3, and some are ready to stretch. The easiest way to stretch from 3 to 4 hours is to spend a week or several on 3½ hours. This gives them time to adjust to slightly longer stretches and possibly one less feed.

Here is a sample routine for a baby on a 3½ hour routine

| | |
|---|---|
| 7:00 | feed (breast/bottle), then awaketime |
| 8:00 | sleep |
| 10:30 | feed, then awaketime |
| 11:30 | sleep |
| 2:00 | feed, then awaketime |
| 3:00 | sleep |
| 5:30 | feed, then awaketime |
| 6:30 | sleep |
| 9:00 | bath, feed, then bed |
| 11:00 | before-bed feed if needed |

Of course these times are flexible and might vary from family to family, so alter the times to fit in with your own family. You may still have a middle-of-the-night feed in there somewhere as well.

Next we will look at those important areas: **feedtime, awaketime, sleeptime.**

## Feedtime

Many mums are going well with their breastfeeding at the three month mark. Baby is growing and feeding well, and sleeping is often going quite well too.

### Keeping Records and Gaining Weight

It is always helpful to check a growth chart – recording your baby's wet/dirty nappies, as well as weight/height gain, frequency of feeds, length of feed times and such. This should give you a fair indication of how he is going with the routine you have been using.

A visit to your Early Childhood Clinic is also helpful to reassure you that things are progressing normally.

> **A happy baby that is sleeping and gaining weight is your best indicator for milk.**

If you are breastfeeding, you will probably notice a significant change in the feel of your breasts at the 3 month mark. Due to hormonal changes your breasts may no longer feel full and uncomfortable during the day, where just a few weeks ago they did. Because of this, many mums worry that they have lost their milk. For lots of mums, however, that is often not the case.

A happy baby that is sleeping and gaining weight is your best indicator for milk, rather than the fullness of your breasts.

*Number of Feeds each Day*

Some mums wonder about the number of feeds they should be giving their baby each day.

This will depend on how far apart his feeds are. If he is happy on 3 hours, then just give him his feeds through the day and any he may wake for during the night. Likewise with 3½ or 4 hourly feeds.

As long as he is happy, sleeping and gaining weight, then the number of feeds will vary from baby to baby. Some need six to seven feeds at this age (or sometimes even more), but some are fine on five and occasionally even four (if they are on four hourly and sleeping ten to eleven hours at night). All this is fine if things are going well.

Bottle fed babies will often have fewer feeds a day than breastfed babies, as you can measure their intake a little better.

You could have most of the feeds regularly at say, 3½ hourly through the day, but then a couple of feeds closer together in the evening (sometimes known as 'cluster feeding'). This may be because your milk supply drops a little towards the end of the day- especially if you have had a busy day.

*Dropping the Evening Feed*

A common concern deals with dropping that last evening feed.

If your baby is struggling to wake for his last feed (around the 10.30pm – 11.00pm mark) and sleeping through till the first morning feed without any problem, then you may consider dropping that last feed.

This happens by gradually feeding them around 15 minutes earlier each night. So for example 10.30pm then 10.15, then 10.00 and so on. Sometimes you might need to stop at a certain time and allow him to 'catch up'. Especially if he starts waking earlier in the morning.

> A cycle of overtiredness, unsettledness, and inefficient feeds can sometimes emerge.

Once your last two feeds are around 1½ - 2 hours apart and your awaketime is melting into the next feed, then you can probably try dropping that feed and popping him straight to bed. This is one time when you might give him a slightly longer awaketime to help that process (eg 1½ hours rather than 1 hour).

Occasionally mums ask about starting solids at this early age. I think three months is usually too early for that. If your baby is a little hungry, then perhaps look at increasing your milk supply to keep up with him, or adding in extra milk feeds.

## Awaketime

If you are trying to keep a good, flexible routine with your baby, then it is really important to be aware of the length of his awaketime. If your awaketime is too long then overtiredness will cause your baby to struggle with his sleeps. Overtired babies also don't feed very well so a cycle of overtiredness, unsettledness, and inefficient feeds can sometimes emerge. Adjusting his awaketime is often a simple and effective way of sorting out some sleep issues.

If you are feeding on a 3 or 3½ hourly routine then it is best to keep your awaketime to an hour or so. If you have already started to stretch to 4 hourly, then that awaketime will likely begin to increase slightly from now on- up to perhaps the 1¼ hour mark.

How will your baby spend his awaketime at this age?

He will probably enjoy watching the activity around him, so popping him somewhere where he can see you is helpful. He will spend some time playing with a toy or watching a mobile, and some time interacting with those around him. Time on the floor, on his back and on his tummy is also a good idea. They love going for walks, having baths and having cuddles.

Again there is no need to over-excite your little baby. Too much stimulation can tire them easily, and lead to unsettled sleeps. Moderation!

## Sleeptime

After their feed, awaketime and play, the next thing to do is go to bed.

**If he is hungry, feed him!**

Many babies of this age still prefer to be wrapped tightly to go to sleep. It does help settle them better as they don't wake themselves up with their own flapping arms. After an hour or so of awaketime, a wrap and goodnight cuddle, it's off to bed.

Most babies are happy to go to sleep, and many 3 month olds are fairly settled and don't generally wake during their sleeps (this might come later...).

If your baby does wake unexpectedly in the middle of a sleep, give him a couple of minutes to see if he will settle himself. Try to resettle him and see if he puts himself back to sleep. If he doesn't and is protesting loudly, it's best to check he isn't hungry. If he is hungry, feed him. Then consider why he seems to be hungry earlier than usual.

> **It is important that baby gets practice at good sleeps throughout the day, so that he will sleep through his sleep cycles during the night as well.**

It is not uncommon for a 3 month old to go through a brief growth spurt.

This might require an extra feed or two for a few days until your milk supply catches up again.

It shouldn't go on for weeks though. If your baby remains unsettled for longer than a week, it could be because your milk supply needs to build up further. Or it could be that extra feeding isn't the answer.

It could also mean that baby has become used to getting up early and is more driven by habit than food. If this is the case, then it might be time to use some resettling techniques (see Chapter Ten).

If your baby starts waking earlier in the morning it could also be a sign of hunger. If so, feed him and examine how you can build up your supply.

One of the symptoms of over tiredness is waking early in the morning as well as through the night. And showing no eagerness to eat like a baby would who is hungry. It is important that baby gets practice at good sleeps throughout the day so that he will sleep through his sleep cycles during the night as well.

# Frequently Asked Questions...

**My baby is 13 weeks old, and I am feeding 3½ - 4 hourly. He is sleeping well, and I am keeping him up for 2 hours of awaketime. My problem is that he just doesn't seem happy – is this normal?**

I suspect your baby is very tired and needs much more sleep!

Even though they seem to be sleeping for so much of the day at this age, this is very normal – and necessary. Don't worry – he will wake up in a couple of months and you will see much more of him ☺.

In the meantime, a awaketime of one hour (or just a little more) is plenty. Even less (around 45-60 minutes or so) if he is still on 3 hourly feeds.

**My baby is 3 months old. He was sleeping quite well at night a few weeks ago, but he is now waking several times during the night. He isn't interested in a feed! I am feeding him between 3 and 4 hourly through the day – depending on when he wakes.**

Apart from hunger issues, another common reason for babies of this age to wake in the night (after sleeping through a few weeks ago) is inconsistent day routine.

For some babies, the feeding pattern needs to be much more predictable than 'between 3 and 4 hourly, depending on when he wakes'. For some babies, it needs to be 3 hourly or 4 hourly. But not an inconsistent mix between the two.

I suggest that you pick a routine that works best for your baby (3, 3½, or 4 hourly), and try very hard to stick to it as consistently as possibly for a few days to see if that helps things at night.

It will mean waking him if he is still asleep at feed time. It will mean consistent awaketimes, that are not too long (45-75 minutes depending on his feed times). It will also mean careful resettling at night – waiting 10 minutes or so to see if he settles. Then going in and picking him up and resettling him before putting him down for another 10-15 minutes or so, until he falls asleep.

If he is still not settling after a few attempts at resettling him then perhaps try to feed him. And try again tomorrow night ☺

## My baby is 3 months old. He is doing well most of the time, with occasional moments of unsettledness. However, I am so tired! How am I going to keep this up for months?

Congratulations on doing so well with your baby, and welcome to Motherhood!

Even though your baby is doing well and sleeping at night, it is still tiring. There is no escaping this! You are a mother now, and that involves 24-hour, round-the-clock care. Thankfully your baby is settled and sleeps well, and will hopefully continue to do so. But for the next, well, twenty years, you will be on duty as mum. They will wake with sickness, wet beds, bad dreams, bad days, and a dozen other reasons for years to come. A flexible routine will reduce the unpredictability of sleeplessness, but it cannot be totally eliminated.

Make sure you get plenty of rest when you can and look after your own physical needs. Accept support from your family and friends and learn to enjoy this precious new life that God has given you.

## My 3 month old suddenly seems extra hungry. Does this mean that I have suddenly lost my milk?

It is not uncommon for a 3 month old baby to go through a brief growth spurt.

This is an opportunity for you to add some extra feeds, which will signal your body to produce more milk to keep up with your baby's growing needs. Once your milk has increased that little bit to keep up with baby, things should settle down again.

If it is a growth spurt, it should last just a few days. If baby is continuing to be unsettled after a week or more, you may consider looking at your milk supply, and ways to build it up further (see Chapter Nine for more tips on building up supply).

## Should I keep wrapping my 12 week old? He seems to fight the wrap.

I do believe that most 3 month olds do better being wrapped while they sleep. They just tend to startle themselves with their own arms when they are left unwrapped, and they usually settle quicker if they are wrapped. In another month or so, that wrapping will not be quite as critical.

If wrapping him is causing more problems for your baby and he seems happy to settle without a wrap, then of course you can stop wrapping. You need to do what is working for you both.

## I am feeding my 3 month old 3½ hourly. But I am struggling to remember his feedtimes. Especially when each day starts at a slightly different time!

If you start your day by writing down your potential feed times (based on that first feed of the morning when he wakes up) and sticking them on the fridge, you will be more likely to remember when you are supposed to be feeding your baby. That way when baby wakes during the day you can quickly check where he is up to in his routine.

**I am having trouble waking my 3 month old for her 10pm feed. However I am worried that if she misses that feed, she will wake in the night again.**

Perhaps it is time to gradually bring that feed forward so that she can drop it altogether.

Try waking her at 9.45pm, then 9.30 and so on until she is going to bed after her earlier feed and sleeping all night. As long as all else is going well with your milk supply and her day sleeps, then it sounds like she might be ready for dropping that last evening feed.

# Three Month Baby Review
*After 3 Months reflect on how baby is going...*

## Weight and Growth
Weight:
Length:

## Feedtime
Duration:      20 mins or under □   20-40 mins □   40-60 mins □

Baby is usually feeding around
        every 2 hrs or less □   2-3 hrs □   3+ hrs □

Any concerns?

Other reflections on feeding...

*if bottle feeding* mls per feed:

## Sleeptime
Baby is going to bed:         awake □   asleep □

Duration of baby's sleep:
    less than 60 mins □   60-90 mins □   90-120 mins □   120+ mins □

Resettling:         most sleeps □   some sleeps □   rarely □

Baby's routine is starting to look like...

Any concerns?

Other reflections on sleeping...

## Awaketime
during awaketime my baby...

**Mum reflections**

The best things about these 3 months have been...


The hardest things about these 3 months have been...


I am thankful to God for...


After 3 months I am feeling...


*Being a wife and mother is not only far and away
the greatest job in the world;
it is also a whole-time job
which takes everything a woman has got to give to it.
William Barclay*


*As a mother comforts her child,
so I'll comfort you.
Isaiah 66:13*

# Chapter Four — Four month olds

4 month olds are so cute!

They are responsive, alert, smiley, and starting to play with their toys. They can hold a rattle, play with their mobile, and some are even sitting up with help, or even alone. Washing baskets and cushions are great for help with this. Occasionally some little ones are biting-at-the-bit and starting to try to crawl. They love to play on their tummies more often, lifting their little heads so they can watch all the action around them.

4 months is also a time of change, meaning lots of questions from mum and dad. Their increased alertness means that they sometimes have trouble staying asleep during their nap times. They just want to be where the action is!

In this chapter we will look at what to do when your 4 month old stops sleeping for his whole nap. We'll also look at why he may seem hungry, building up and maintaining your milk supply, and a few other bits and pieces that crop up around now.

Firstly here is a sample routine for a 4 month old. Of course, the times are flexible and may change from family to family. But it will give you an idea of where to start if your routine is wobbly.

This sample is based on a 4 hourly routine:

| | |
|---|---|
| 7:00 | feed (breast/bottle), then awaketime |
| 8:15 | sleep |
| 11:00 | feed, then awaketime |
| 12:15 | sleep |
| 3:00 | feed, then awaketime |
| 4:15 | sleep |
| 7:00 | bath, feed, then awaketime |
| 8:30 | sleep |
| 10:30 | top up feed if needed, then bed for the night |

Next we will look at those important areas: **feedtime, awaketime, sleeptime** and then resettling and frequently asked questions.

## Feedtime

Many 4 month olds are ready to go closer to 4 hourly feeds by now if they haven't already. If your milk supply is going well (or you are bottle feeding), then you may consider moving to around 4 hourly feeds.

*Stretching Feed Times*

How do you know if baby is ready to stretch or if your milk supply will keep up?

It is always helpful to check a growth chart – recording your baby's wet/dirty nappies, as well as weight/height gain, frequency of feeds, length of feed times and such. This should give you a fair indication of how he is going with the routine you have been using.

A visit to your Early Childhood Clinic is also helpful to reassure you that things are progressing normally.

A baby may be hungry if he is regularly waking early for feeds – and then feeding enthusiastically. If he is suddenly waking in the night again and taking full feeds, then it may mean a growth spurt or milk supply issue to work on.

*When Milk Supply Drops*

Often mums are back into their busy lives at four months– shopping, meeting friends, playgroup, exercising, cleaning house, working and a stack of other things. They feel great but their baby sometimes gets left behind.

**If you are breastfeeding, then you must slow down and look after yourself!**

How can you build up your supply if it has dropped a little?

If you are breastfeeding, then you must slow down and look after yourself!

You need to drink lots of water and consume enough calories to produce enough milk to feed your baby. Some mums struggle with this. If this is you, then you may need to make some changes to help your milk supply build up again. Have an afternoon rest, go to bed earlier, drink more water, eat well and add extra feeds as needed.

If you are worried about your supply dropping, pumping after feeds is an effective way to increase your supply – just pump for a few minutes after a feed, store in the fridge and offer it to him after the next breastfeed. You can do this up to three times a day for around three-five days to notice a difference.

Other temporary methods of boosting supply include giving a top up feed before bed in the afternoon/evening, or adding another late evening feed if you aren't already doing one.

Sometimes mums are feeding quite well on a 3 hourly routine and a little reluctant for that to change in case they come across problems of supply or unsettledness. If you are happy feeding at 3 hourly, then of course you can continue for a while longer. Problems often arise as they get bigger however, because they are so much more alert. This affects their sleeping patterns, because their awaketimes get longer and their sleeps get shorter. This can lead in turn to night waking because they don't get to practice moving through their sleep cycles during the day (more on sleep later).

Most mums who have a good milk supply can consider gradually moving to a 4 hourly routine with their babies at around this age. Mums who are bottle-feeding could also consider increasing those feed times to 4 hourly if they haven't already.

If you are breastfeeding you may have noticed your baby feeding in a much shorter time. This is common as baby gets stronger and more efficient at sucking.

If your baby is a 'slow coach' however, you may want to limit his feeding time (perhaps to 10/15 minutes a side) so that he can have more playtime after his feed. Most babies soon figure out that it is worth their while to feed more efficiently. My little Madeline was always a slow coach!

I always suggest to continue feeding from both breasts to give adequate stimulation and maintain supply.

Feeding should take anywhere from 5-10 minutes (for those faster feeders like my Oliver), to 30 minutes (for those slow coaches).

*Dropping the Late Feed*

Another thing that you may choose to think about if you haven't already, is dropping the late evening feed. Bring back the time of that last feed (for example, 10.30pm) 15 minutes each night until there is a gap of 2 hours or so between the last two feeds. You would probably not even have another sleeptime before you feed them again. Then once you are comfortable that they can stretch, put them to bed at the end of a awaketime without that last feed.

If they start waking early in the morning, you can just keep that last feed time until baby is happy stretching to the morning start time again. For example, baby may do fine at sleeping all night until you hit a last feed of 9pm. Then he suddenly doesn't stretch! Just wait on that time for a few days until he is stretching again.

This whole process usually takes a week or two, and you can do this from around 3 months old onwards. If your supply has been iffy, then it is probably best to wait until it has established again.

If your milk supply is unstable or if this late feed gives you peace of mind, then feel free to continue with it for as long as you wish.

## Awaketime

> **If you are trying to keep a good routine with your baby, then it is important to be aware of the length of his awaketime.**

### How long is Awaketime?

If you are trying to keep a good routine with your baby then it is important to be aware of the length of his awaketime. Too much awaketime and you risk an overtired baby who struggles to sleep well. Too little awaketime and your baby will be frustrated, wake early for feeds (thus upsetting the feed/play/sleep routine) and sleep poorly.

If you are using a 4 hourly routine, then around 1¼ hours or so is usually plenty of awaketime for this age. He may have one period of the day where he stays up a little longer. This awaketime will gradually increase as he gets older. At 6 months he'll have around 2 hours of awaketime and 2 hours of sleeptime.

For a 4 month old on a 3 hourly routine, 1 hour of awaketime should be enough or he won't get extended sleep.

Some mums regularly wait for 'tired signs' (including jerky movements, clenched fists and screwing up face) before putting baby to bed. While tired signs are very helpful and shouldn't be ignored, it is helpful to know that some babies really don't show tired signs until they are well and truly over-tired. Once your baby is over-tired, he will often go to sleep quite well initially but then wake into his sleep and struggle to resettle himself.

It works best to put them to bed after around the same amount of awaketime each feed cycle, rather than regularly waiting for the tired signs to appear.

If you apply a consistent and appropriate awaketime length with your four month old, you can avoid his chronic over-tiredness.

*The Three Phases of Awaketime*

> **Play alone, play near mum, play with mum.**

After your baby's feed and burping, you can look at the three play phases of awaketime.

The first phase is **playing alone:**

Give him some playtime on the floor. This will give him an opportunity to stretch and kick his legs and arms and allow any trapped wind to escape. At 4 months they love to play with mobiles and to hold toys in their hand – even if still a little awkwardly. They enjoy sitting up and watching the family- just waiting for someone to pay attention to them!

A playpen can also be a part of this phase of awaketime. Use it for a short time (5-10 minutes) twice a day (morning and afternoon).

The next phase of their awaketime is **playing near mum:**

He can play with his toys while watching mum from a short distance. He can look quietly around the room, or spend time jumping in a Jolly Jumper. All this is in the sight of mum, with occasional interaction - just not undivided attention.

The third phase is **playing with mum**·

This means cuddles, reading and singing with mum. It is handy to finish their awaketime with this one. Enjoy playing with him if you are stretching a awaketime a little, or if baby needs a little settling or calming before bedtime.

Keep it all in balance, and enjoy your baby's unique personality.

Too much rapid change in activity and some can feel slightly overwhelmed. Too little change and others get bored.

This is a lovely age for taking out and about for short times. They are generally responsive to friendly strangers and eager to see the world around them.

Keep your outings in check- three to four outings a week are usually plenty for our little babies. Too much busyness can add to a general unsettledness in your baby A stable, consistent home routine is well worth it now.

Avoid awaketime during the night or very early in the morning. You want your baby to know the difference between playtime and sleeptime, and night and day. When you do need to feed him during the night, try to feed him and put him back to bed without any play.

## Sleeptime

After he has been fed and had some playtime, it is time for bed.

Some babies are showing signs of tiredness by the end of awaketime. Other babies look like they could go on forever- they seem so happy to be up and playing. Nevertheless they need to sleep – they are still only little babies.

## Wrapping

For these first four months, he has probably appreciated being wrapped to go to sleep. However, many mums find now that their little baby has become a Houdini! They often just don't want or need to be wrapped tightly as they did when they were newborn.

Sometimes a time of transition can help by gradually wrapping him loosely. The wrap becomes a 'cue' that it is sleeptime, rather than a means of restricting his arms and legs.

If your baby still loves to be wrapped, then go ahead and wrap him for longer if you wish! My little Jemima did love to be wrapped until she was about 6 months old.

## Going to Sleep

Most babies that have been on a flexible routine from birth will go down to sleep quite well. Some still have a little protest cry, but by now you should be more aware of your baby's normal behaviour at sleeptime.

**Awareness of baby's normal behaviour is important so that you can hear when he is behaving differently, and respond appropriately.**

Awareness of baby's normal behaviour is important so that you can hear when he is behaving differently, and respond appropriately. Most of mine were very happy to go quickly off to sleep at this age, except for my Elliot – he protested every sleep! This was his normal however, and I just let him have a minute or two of protest before he was fine and sleeping soundly.

*Interrupted Sleeps*

Times of interrupted sleeps are rather common around four months. This is frustrating especially for those mums whose babies have been settled up to now.

> **They are processing their little world, and it is much too exciting to sleep through!**

Sometimes a baby wakes during a sleeptime and stays awake for some time (up to 30 minutes) without crying. Mum discovers that he is wriggling around and watching his room or overhanging mobile, rather than going back to sleep. Sometimes after being awake for a while, he might begin to start fussing again as he gets tired.

This time of mid-sleep wakefulness is usually fairly short lived, and they only seem to keep it up for a week or two. I have always guessed that while they were younger they were not especially interested in their surroundings. Now at 4 months they are processing their little world. And it is much too exciting to sleep through! Possibly this is a time to put that mobile away for a month or two.

Once he starts fussing, check the time to see how long he has been crying (it often seems longer than it really is). If he is still fussy after 10-15 minutes, try to resettle him (see over the page for tips).

Another problem with interrupted sleep happens when baby wakes out of a deep sleep to cry. He may only have been asleep for 30-45 minutes.

This commonly happens around 45 minutes into a sleeptime because they are following a cycle of deep and active sleep. As they reach an active period of sleep – around the 40-45 minute mark, they come out of their sleep and wake to cry. Their cry can range from fussy on and off, to full-on bellow!

The first thing to do is stop and check the clock. How long is it since my baby went to sleep? Is baby ready for a feed?

You should always consider that your baby may be hungry.

From time to time, they do get hungry unexpectedly.

Perhaps he is going through a growth spurt. Perhaps you have been ill or busy rushing around and your milk supply has been affected. Perhaps he has a cold and is extra thirsty.

He may tell you he's hungry by feeding enthusiastically- even though it is earlier than you were expecting. Consider that your milk supply may need a boost to keep up with his needs.

If you are noticing a pattern that your baby is consistently waking during sleeps and doesn't seem hungry, then maybe it's time to consider some alternatives.

It is common for 4 month old babies to become over-stimulated after long awaketimes, or too much activity outside the home. If this is happening in your house, then you could make some changes to baby's awaketime and general out-and-about activities. It is surprising how many babies fall back into routine once the issue of over-stimulation has been addressed.

If you have decided that baby is not hungry but just needs to learn to go back to sleep, then it is time to have a Resettling Plan.

## Resettling

This resettling plan will need to be consistent in order to be most effective. Let me share with you my Resettling Plan - a plan successful with my own babies, and many, many others too!

> **To successfully resettle your baby, it is important to have a consistent plan.**

Make sure your baby is just needing to learn to resettle himself, and isn't hungry or stuck. Usually they'll give a different cry if they are stuck.

Wait 10 minutes or so after first hearing him cry out during his sleeptime.

Then go in and pick him up. Pat or rub his back soothingly until he calms down. He may calm down almost instantly, or it may take a few minutes. Very often he will look around with bright eyes, sometimes even smiling- so delighted to be up and ready for action!

While it is tempting to get him up for a play, many mothers discover that if they do get their baby up at that point, he will only remain happy for a short time. They often become fussy again rather quickly because they need more sleep!

> **When mum goes in every 10-15 minutes or so while he is fussing, she can continually assess what he is up to.**

After he is calm, put him straight back down and softly tell him that it is sleep time now. Then leave the room and wait around 10-15 minutes before going back in.

Most babies will protest loudly at that decision!

If there has been some unsettledness for quite a few days already, baby may persist with crying right up to the next feed time. You may need to go in every 10-15 minutes or so for quite some time! This is rare though, and most babies will calm down with just a little fussing on and off until they fall asleep.

When you go in every 10-15 minutes or so while he is fussing, you can continually assess what he is up to. You are part of solving the problem.

Perhaps you go in and your baby is just fussing or grizzling (rather than crying). You may feel that picking him up might only wake him up further. You can wait a few more minutes and check again, or just give him a soothing pat.

There may be occasions, particularly if he is unwell, that you need to spend a little longer cuddling or rocking baby to calm him down so he can get off to sleep. This is fine.

If you regularly rock, bounce or swing your baby to help him get to sleep, you may have troubles down the track. He may learn to depend on you to get to sleep. But it is not fun to be trying to rock your growing baby to sleep during the night (night after night). This type of resettling is also more stimulating, which only prolongs the cycle of over-tiredness.

> **The key is for mum to be consistent with her resettling.**

If you are attempting to implement a tighter routine involving resettling, then be prepared for a few days of hard work. Especially if you have had a few days (or even weeks) of unsettledness! Your baby will not be happy with the new rules at first. But most mums find that after three-five days or so, their babies are much happier to go to bed. And happy to sleep for their entire sleeptimes-mostly!

The key is for mum to be consistent with her resettling.

Perhaps you have tried to implement a routine. You have faithfully followed the resettling guidelines. You are sure that your baby is not hungry, yet after a week you are still having no success. For your own piece of mind it will be helpful to check with a doctor. You just might want to be sure there is no underlying reason (like an ear infection) that may be contributing to your baby's distress.

Frequently Asked Questions...

My four month old baby is only sleeping for half his sleeptime. He doesn't seem hungry – should I just get him up until the next feed?

There are a number of questions for parents to ask themselves when this begins to happen.

Is this a *feeding/hunger* problem, or a *sleep/routine* problem?

If you suspect a *feeding/hunger* problem, then feed your baby- but have a think about why baby is waking hungry earlier than previously. Is he going through a growth spurt? Has your milk supply dropped?

If you do suspect a drop in supply, then there are some tips for building it up again in Chapter Nine.

There may other reasons for his unusual hunger. He may be going through a growth spurt. He may have been unwell. Or there may be some other reason for him needing some extra food. Feed him early for a few days until he is no longer unusually hungry, and then you can get back to a routine that is suiting everyone.

If you suspect a *sleeping/routine* problem (a common one at this age), then you will probably find that your baby is quite happy to get up after a short sleep, and doesn't really want a full feed. After a short play time, or even after the next feed, he may become tired and grumpy. He may also start waking in the night, unable to resettle himself.

Sometimes they fall asleep straight after the next feed, and then wake early again. This can become a tricky cycle of sleep/play/feed instead of feed/play/sleep.

If this is happening in your house, then consider what other things might be happening in his day.

Are his awaketimes too long? The most common reason for unsettled babies, aside from hunger and growth spurts, is long awaketimes. Especially around the 4 month mark. Over-stimulation really doesn't produce a happy, well sleeping baby! Try putting him to bed earlier as a start, to allow him some longer sleep times.

Likewise, if you have been putting him to bed too soon after a feed, then increase his awaketimes a little until things get sorted out again.

Are your days too busy? If you are out and about too often in the week, this can also be unsettling for a young baby.

Do you have a lot of visually stimulating things in his room? Mobiles? Posters? These can be too much for some babies – put them away for a short time.

Are there any other things happening in your home? Mother-in-law staying? Just moved house? Baby and/or family members sick? Something else unusual? All these big events impact baby, often with him being unable to resettle during a sleeptime.

## My five month old is sleeping well at night, but regularly waking early for feeds during the day. I am giving him a one hour awaketime.

At five months, it is probably time to start extending his awaketime. He is more alert now, and needing that extra time awake, to work off some energy. Try giving him a awaketime of 1½ hours or so (perhaps even a little longer at some cycles), and see if he sleeps through to the next feed better.

**My 4 month old is waking around 45 minutes into his nap every time. I have tried getting him up for a feed, but he isn't hungry. Should I just let him cry until his next feed?**

No. It is most likely that your baby is waking because of interrupted sleep cycles. At that 45 minute mark, he is probably waking up during the active sleep stage.

I suggest giving him about 10 minutes to see if he will settle on his own. Listen to his cry. Is it loud and screamy or on and off ? Decide if you need to go in and pick him up for a settling cuddle, or allow him another minute or two to see if he will fall asleep on his own.

If he is crying persistently, give him a soothing cuddle until he calms down. Then pop him back to bed for another 10 or 15 minutes, to have another try at settling back to sleep, If he is still crying after that time, try resettling again.

You can continue to resettle like this right u[ until his next feed. Or you can give up after a few tries and have another go next time. Often a baby will protest right up until the next feed the first time mum attempts consistently resettle. Most will start to self-settle from then on.

If things have gotten out of whack in your house, you may need to be persistent for a several days to get back on track again. If this is the first day of resettling, you may need to give him lots of extra cuddles before he pushes through these sleep cycles.

If baby is grizzling in an on-and-off way, it may be because he is getting tired and is close to falling asleep on his own. It might be better to leave him for a few extra minutes, rather than picking him up and waking him up again.

If all else is well with his feeds, health and weight gain, this type of resettling for a few days should have no long lasting effect on baby. And it will probably help him get over this bump of sleep unsettledness!

## My 4 month old seems to spend part of his sleep time watching his mobile. He isn't crying, but he isn't sleeping either. Is this normal?

It isn't uncommon for babies of this age to spend some of their sleep time awake. They are just more alert now than they were a month ago!

There may be nothing that you need to do about this for now. They may have a little cry after being awake for a while, because they do get tired eventually and cry to get themselves settled back to sleep. This is usually fine. A few minutes of crying to resettle is OK.

If you have a particularly attractive mobile above his bed, it might be an idea to put it away for a month or two. This will reduce the distractions in his room.

## I have just started putting my 5 month old in the playpen. She cries for the whole hour! What should I do?

An hour is way too long for a 5 month old to be in the playpen! Better to start with 5 minutes. Once she is happy for those 5 minutes, you can extend it to 10, then 15. However she probably won't be happy in the playpen for a whole hour until she is bigger.

## Should I start giving my four month old baby solids?

While it is a little young (6 months is probably an average time to start solids), you may consider starting some solids around this time. If you have a good milk supply but your baby is still hungry, you can start with some rice cereal, or something similar. Offer it once a day to start, and then gradually build up to three meals a day.

If baby gobbles up every mouthful, then great! If he then starts sleeping better, and seems more settled, then all is good. If baby spits out his food or is not interested in eating at all, then it is probably too early. Wait until he is six months or so and try again.

If baby is settled and seems to be thriving on your milk, then there is no need to rush into solids just yet.

**My friend's baby is the same age as mine – 4 months – and is eating solids. I tried it with my baby, but she is not interested. Should I try giving her solids before her breastfeed?**

If your baby is not interested in solids after her feed, then she is probably not ready. If you give her solids before her breastfeed, she may not drink much milk. This will mean that your supply might start to flag. Better to keep up your supply now, and offer solids in another month or two (after a breastfeed!).

There is more information on introducing solids in the next chapter.

# Four Month Baby Review
*After 4 Months reflect on how baby is going...*

## Weight and Growth
Weight:
Length:

## Feedtime
Duration:　　　　20 mins or under ☐ 20-40 mins ☐ 40-60 mins ☐

· Baby is usually feeding around

every 2 hrs or less ☐ 2-3 hrs ☐ 3+ hrs ☐

Any concerns?

Other reflections on feeding...

*if bottle feeding* mls per feed:

## Sleeptime
Baby is going to bed:　　　　　　　　awake ☐ asleep ☐

Duration of baby's sleep:
less than 60 mins ☐ 60-90 mins ☐ 90-120 mins ☐ 120+ mins ☐

Resettling:　　　　　　　most sleeps ☐ some sleeps ☐ rarely ☐

Baby's routine is looking like...

Any concerns?

Other reflections on sleeping...

## Awaketime
during awaketime my baby...

**Mum reflections**

The best things about these 4 months have been...

The hardest things about these 4 months have been...

I am thankful to God for...

After 4 months I am feeling...

*A mother's love is like a circle, it has no beginning and no ending.*
*It keeps going around and around ever expanding,*
*touching everyone who comes in contact with it.*
*Art Urban*

*I call on you, my God, for you will answer me;*
*turn your ear to me and hear my prayer.*
*Psalm 17:6*

Chapter Five　　　　　　　# Six month olds

What treasures 6 month olds are!

Many are starting to sit up. A few are even starting to crawl. They are smiley, and starting to bubble over with personality. They love to be played with, and to be the centre of attention.

In this chapter we will look at 6 month olds and feedtime, routine, resettling, awaketime activities and frequently asked questions.

Firstly, a sample routine for a 6 month old:

| | |
|---|---|
| 7:00 | wake up, feed: breastfeed/bottle, then cereal if giving solids. Playpen and play |
| 9:00 | nap |
| 11:00 | feed (followed by lunch) and awaketime |
| 1:00 | nap |
| 3:00 | feed and dinner. Playpen and play. |
| 5:00 | nap |
| 7:00 | bath, feed, play |
| 8:00 / 8:30 | bed |
| 9:30(ish) | another top up feed if needed |

**Feedtime**

Often mums feel that they need to have all the feed times lined up to adult mealtimes by this age. But this is the age that babies **start** to gradually extend their routines. Their mealtimes will be fully lined up with the rest of the family at around 12 months.

77

*Keeping Up Supply*

Many mums are breastfeeding quite comfortably by this time, and their babies are starting to look quite roly-poly. Or sometimes just very long.

But from time to time mums worry about their baby's growth, and their own milk supply. Use growth charts to make sure your baby is gaining weight normally, or check in regularly with your local clinic sister if you are at all concerned. Once a month clinic visits are usually enough, unless there are underlying problems that need to be revisited.

Perhaps you are worried about your milk supply dropping. Pump after feeds for a few days or or add the late night feed back in. These are effective way to increase your supply.

**Now is not the time to go on a low fat, low carbs diet, coupled with a morning jog and a visit to the gym five times a week!**

If your supply is still struggling, you can also offer a top up feed before one or more sleeps- or even before every sleep, until it is re-established (usually a week or so). Hopefully this will only be temporary until your supply is re-established again.

Remember to drink your water, keep your own calorie intake well up, and exercise in moderation. Poor water intake, poor calorie intake and too much exercising (or even running around doing too much), can all contribute to a low milk supply. Now is not the time to go on a low fat, low carbs diet, coupled with a morning jog and a visit to the gym five times a week!

Mums with older children can also suffer from 'supply dips'. They are running around with school, preschool, afternoon activities and such. Slow down and enjoy this precious time with your new baby! Sometimes mum finds vitamin (or even recommended herbal) supplements helpful to give a flagging milk supply a boost.

Some mums, for various reasons, are bottle-feeding. That's ok. You are not a bad mother for bottle-feeding. Your baby will still grow up to be healthy and happy. Just remember not to leave baby in bed with a bottle, for the sake of his dental health.

*Introducing Solids*

Many babies at around six months will be ready to start some solids. You can start with rice cereal once a day, gradually increasing to three times a day. Then you can add in pureed vegetables or fruit. Try to give solids soon after a milk feed, rather than an hour or two later.

Remember: **always** give milk before solids! This will help maintain your milk supply.

It is not uncommon for mums to try giving solids at 6 months, only to find bub spits it out! This doesn't mean he didn't like the taste, but more likely that his reflexes are just not ready for solids yet. If he continues to spit out the food, then perhaps try again in a few weeks.

> **Remember: always give milk before solids! This will help maintain your milk supply.**

Some days baby will refuse his food. Some days he will gobble it up. There is no need to fix him something different if he has refused his meal. If he is hungry, he will eat. If he is not particularly hungry this time, he will eat better next mealtime. If you start worrying about what he may or may not like, you will go bananas trying to keep up with him! Try not to feel that you need to accommodate all your baby's apparent tastes in food - you may end up training him to be a fussy eater!

## Routine

2 hours of awaketime, then 2 hours of sleep.

*Two-up, Two-down*

A handy routine guide to remember at 6 months is: two up, two down. That is, 2 hours of awaketime, then 2 hours of sleep. Some babies will do ok with just 1½ hours of sleep and a short playtime before the next feed. In fact, many babies at six months are quite happy to have a short play before their feed, even after a nice long sleep. They are just getting that little bit bigger.

Sometimes mums give their baby a very long awaketime, and he is over tired. Or a very short awaketime, and he is frustrated at being in bed too long. This can disrupt the cycle of feed/wake/sleep.

Try to keep to approximately the same times every day so that the baby feels secure in the routine. Between the ages of 6 and 12 months, the feed times will *gradually* spread out more. They will line up with regular breakfast/lunch/dinner mealtimes for the rest of the family by around 12 months. That mid-afternoon feed is the one most likely to eventually stretch out to dinner.

Each nap should be around 1½-2 hours long. If he wakes quite early during a nap and you are sure he isn't hungry or dirty, then resettling him will help him to learn to fall back to sleep on his own.

The third nap (around 5pm) will gradually shorten over the next few months, and then drop altogether around 9-10 months of age.

It is good to aim for some flexibility, as strict clock watching is often unrealistic. Too much flexibility however, and babies become uncertain of their routine, and more unsettled.

If baby is doing really well on this routine, you may feel ready to start extending it a little. You might start with the first stretch between breakfast and lunch. Try stretching his awaketime by 15 minutes. A play for 15 minutes or so after his nap before lunch will also help stretch his routine.

## Resettling

If baby is truly struggling to resettle during naps, and feeding and routine are ok, then you may need to consider resettling techniques.

The key is always to be as consistent as possible.

I usually suggest going in every 10-15 minutes or so to pick up, soothe, and put baby back down for another 10-15 minute stretch. Sometimes you may need to spend quite a few minutes calming him down if he is really screamy – be patient.

If you suspect he is in pain/not feeling well etc, then get him checked out for reassurance.

Consistency with resettling usually works after five days or so. The first day is the hardest until baby gradually works out that he is supposed to be sleeping. By the end of a week, most babies are sleeping much better, with maybe one protest sleep cycle/day.

Now and then he may fuss on and off through to the next feed. Sometimes he may stay awake but happy. But mostly he will learn to go back to sleep.

**Remember:
we are training baby
to put himself back
to sleep on his own.**

Remember: we are training baby to put himself back to sleep on his own.

This skill will help for night time waking also. If baby has been waking at night, then he will nearly always have a day waking problem that needs to be addressed first (whether it be feeding related, or routine/resettling problems). Once he can settle himself during the day, the night usually sorts itself out.

Another common question around six months relates to **dummies** (or pacifiers).

If your baby has been using one from birth and it is not a problem, then I don't see a major problem with a 6 month old having a dummy. If however, it has come to an issue of enslavement, then it helps to think through how you want to use (or eliminate) the dummy. Having to go in fifty times to put it back in every time it falls out may be considered a frustrating problem needing address!

> **Playpens, as part of a routine, are very useful tools that help little ones to have some focused play.**

Some folks go Cold Turkey. Throw out the dummy and manage an unhappy day or two until baby learns to settle himself.

Other folks do a Slow Wean. Limiting the dummy to going to bed initially, but not putting it back if it falls out. Or putting baby to bed without the dummy, but putting it in to resettle if baby wakes during his nap and won't resettle. Or using it for day sleeps, but not night time. Or the other way around.

Some parents only ever buy newborn size dummies, so that baby finds it too difficult to keep sucking, and gives up naturally.

Some folks are happy to use dummies for longer, and that is fine too.

## Awaketime Activities

### Playpens

Playpens used as part of a routine, are very useful to help little ones to have some focused play. It is ideal to start at around four-six months (sometimes even earlier if there are older siblings, for self-protection!).

You could gradually work up to 30-45 minutes playpen time after breakfast, and another 15-20 minutes or so in the afternoon after feeding. These times work best because baby is well fed and well rested, and much more likely to enjoy this time playing alone.

Some babies like my Rosie, are content to play happily in a playpen that is in the living room, with household activity not disturbing them. While others like my Elliot, need to be isolated a little more from the hustle and bustle of family life. You can try moving the playpen into a spare room, bedroom, or hidden in a corner a little more. See what works best for baby.

At this age, a mobile or a few toys are adequate company, depending on how mobile they are. Few are better than too many, which can be overwhelming to a little one.

Start with 5 minutes and cheerfully pull him out at the end (regardless of how happy or unhappy he is), and then gradually extend it. Sometimes it is helpful for them to listen to some background music.

*Other Awaketime Activities*

Other awaketime activities for this age group include walks, floor play (back and tummy), bathing, sitting in rocker chair with mobile, book or toy, playing in the high chair, or just watching people potter around the house.

**Give him plenty of cuddles and interactive play.**

Give him plenty of cuddles and interactive play.

Watch out that he doesn't become so dependent on being carried around that he is unable to spend any time alone.

Remember too that while stimulation is good, too much means a grumpy baby who will struggle to stay asleep during nap-time. Over-stimulation can also contribute to sudden night waking.

Balance!

Frequently Asked Questions...

**My 6 month old baby is not happy after a feed, and is waking early from his naps. My milk seems to be ok – what can I do?**

At this age, it may be worth considering introducing solids. Start with one meal a day – some rice cereal, for example – after a breastfeed. Over a few days or weeks, you can increase those solids to three meals a day, and include some pureed vegetables.

If your baby is not able to swallow his food, or is constantly poking his tongue out, he may not be ready yet. Wait for a week or so and try again.

It is always worth considering if life has simply become too busy for your little baby. Lots of activity and busy going-out days may cause him to be unsettled. A few days to catch up on sleep and quiet routine at home can also work wonders.

If baby *is* happy during his awaketime, but still waking a little early from naps, this is usually fine. As long as he has had a good sleep (1½-2 hours), then he can have a little play before his next feed.

## My 6 month old baby doesn't seem to be gaining weight as fast as she used to. My doctor is happy, but should I be worried about this?

In those first few weeks and months, a baby's weight gain is quite rapid – much more so than now. If she were to gain weight at the same rate as a newborn, she would be enormous at this point!

Is she looking well? Sleeping and feeding well? Happy during her awaketime? Growing out of her clothes? Then she is probably fine. As long as your clinic sister or doctor is happy with her weight, then there is probably no need to worry.

## My 6 month old baby wants to be carried around all the time. When I put her down, she just cries until I pick her up again. Now I am getting a sore back! What can I do?

If your baby is healthy and well, then there should be no need for her to be carried around constantly by you. Some mothers prefer to carry their babies around - you could use a sling for that if you wanted to, to ease the pressure on your back.

If you don't wish to carry her around all day, then now is a good time to consider breaking this habit that you have both gotten into.

Certainly you should feel free to carry her around sometimes, and there is no reason why you can't play with her on your knee and such. But carrying her around all day is different. She is only getting heavier, and will learn to rely on being carried long past the time it has ceased to be fun for you.

Consider whether she is getting enough sleep. Perhaps working on her sleeps will help her to remain happier during her awaketime.

What about her meals? Is she eating well, or do you need to work on building up your milk supply and/or increasing her solids?

Lastly, have a re-think about planning her awaketime, especially in regards to those three areas: time with mum, time near mum, and time alone. Persist with using the playpen twice a day (even if she isn't especially happy – just shorten that time to 5 minutes and gradually build it up again). Make use of the highchair for some of her awaketime – she can watch you potter in the kitchen, while playing with a toy or book. Have you tried a Jolly Jumper? This can be used once a day during awaketime, especially if it is placed somewhere where she can watch you. Or even pop her in her pram for a little while, with a toy, perhaps while you hang out the washing.

While it can be easy to opt for carrying her every time she grizzles, it is probably going to be worth breaking that habit in the long run, even if it does take some time. Try to identify the causes for her unhappiness, and search for alternative answers.

## Should I be making all my own baby food for my 6 month old? Or can I give her tinned baby food?

Tins and jars of commercial baby food are very convenient. They are easy to grab when you are going out, and require no preparation, defrosting, or heating up. There is a wide range of flavours and brands to chose from.

These tinned foods will never be as fresh as homemade baby food, though. If you can, consider preparing your own baby food – vegetables, rice, pasta – mash/puree, and freeze in ice cube trays. This makes it easier to defrost when dinner-time approaches.

It is really up to you. When you make your own food, you can be sure of what ingredients have gone into it. It costs very little – often just mashing up a little extra left over from your own dinner. Shop-bought food, while convenient, can end up being quite expensive!

## My 6 month old baby rather likes her dummy. However, if it falls out in her sleep, she goes bananas! What can I do?

There comes a time when we need to re-think that dummy. When we start dreaming about reams of masking tape to keep it in, it is time to do something drastic!

If your baby has had free access to her dummy, it may be time to gradually restrict her 'dummy time'. You can start with saving it only for bed (rather than whenever she fusses during her awaketime), and for outings.

Then perhaps you could decide to give her the dummy as she goes to sleep initially, but refuse to replace it if it falls out.

Or perhaps you will take it away altogether! Either way, she will not be happy to have her treasured dummy disappear, and you will most likely have a few unhappy days of resettling her during her sleeps. Once it is gone for good, though, it will be worth it!

## I have read about 'blanket time' and would like to start doing it with my 7 month old. How do I start?

Blanket time means teaching your little one to stay and play on a blanket (or sheet, or mat) with a few toys, without wandering off. This is quite a good age to start this – before they become too mobile.

Start by popping him on the blanket with some toys to play with. Keep an eye on him (without hovering), so that if he starts to crawl off the blanket, you can reinforce the boundaries. You might do this by saying "no", and tapping the edge of the blanket, to indicate that going past that point is not allowed.

You would probably only do this for 5 or 10 minutes to start, and then gradually build up to 20-30 minutes. Try to practice every day or two, and you will find that he soon learns what is required of him. It is a very handy tool for those times when you really would love him to play quietly in a small space for a time (like at church, or sport practice etc).

## I have only just discovered the idea of using a flexible routine with my baby. Things have been rather chaotic here for the last 6 months – how am I going to get my baby in a routine?

It is not impossible to come in late and try to put your baby on a flexible routine, but it will take a little hard work.

Probably the first place to start is to write down what a normal day looks like now, so that you can see on paper where you may need to make some changes. Once you can see what you have been doing, then have a look at where you would like to end up with a routine for your baby, in terms of possible feeding and sleeping times.

You will most likely need to shorten some awaketimes, and stretch out some sleeps, which will involve some resettling (see Chapter Ten). Make sure that your milk supply is keeping up (if you are breastfeeding – see Chapter Nine). Start with one part of the day (the mornings are often best), and gradually add the other parts of your day, so that after a week or two, you can see a more consistent routine starting to come together. It is going to take some time, so be patient.

Your baby may seem unhappy for a few days, but will quickly settle into the new plan for the day, and you should start to see a happier baby!

# Six Month Baby Review
*After 6 Months reflect on how baby is going...*

## Weight and Growth
Weight:
Length:

## Feedtime
Duration:  20 mins or under ☐ 20-40 mins ☐  40-60 mins ☐

Baby is usually feeding around

every 2 hrs or less ☐  2-3 hrs ☐  3+ hrs ☐

Baby has started solids?
Any concerns?

Other reflections on feeding...

*if bottle feeding* mls per feed:

## Sleeptime
Baby is going to bed:                          awake ☐  asleep ☐

Duration of baby's sleep:
less than 60 mins ☐  60-90 mins ☐  90-120 mins ☐  120+ mins ☐

Resettling:               most sleeps ☐  some sleeps ☐  rarely ☐

Baby's routine looks like...

Any concerns?

Other reflections on sleeping...

## Awaketime
during awaketime my baby...

**Mum reflections**

The best things about these 6 months have been...

The hardest things about these 6 months have been...

I am thankful to God for...

After 6 months I am feeling...

*My mother was the most beautiful woman I ever saw.*
*All I am I owe to my mother. I attribute all my success in life to the moral,*
*intellectual and physical education I received from her.*
*George Washington*

*But those who trust in the Lord will find new strength.*
*They will soar high on wings like eagles.*
*Isaiah 40:31*

# Chapter Six

# Nine month olds

9 month olds are such a joy!

Some are crawling, and a few are even walking. Most are eating solids, and enjoying spending time in the high chair.

For many parents, this is the first month of needing to be more direct in regards to the word "no", as their little ones begin to explore their world. It is a time of many questions, as our little ones start to become more people-like, and blossom in personality.

Over the years I have answered many questions about 9 month olds. It does seem to be a time of rapid change and new challenges.

In this chapter, we will look at the routine of a 9 month old, as well as the three main areas of their day: feedtime, awaketime and sleeptime. Then we will discuss weaning, and some frequently asked questions.

Here is a sample routine for a 9 month old:

| | |
|---|---|
| 7:00 | wake, feed (breast/bottle), breakfast, playpen etc. |
| 10:00 | nap |
| 11:30 / 12:00 | feed, lunch, play etc |
| 2:00 - 4:00 | nap |
| 5:00 | feed, dinner, playpen/play |
| 6:00 - 6:30 | nap? |
| 7:00 | bath, before-bed feed, play |
| 7:30 / 8:00 | bed |

Of course, this can be varied to suit your own lifestyle, but it gives you something to start with.

## Feedtime

You may have been feeding 4 hourly (or even more frequently) up till now. If you haven't started stretching those feed times, then now is a good time. Your baby will most likely be on three regular mealtimes (plus a possible evening milk feed) by around 12 months.

### Keeping Up Supply

While you are still breastfeeding, always nurse **before** any solids. This is important to maintain your milk supply, so that you can continue to breastfeed for longer. Then give a solid meal soon after, if possible (rather than an hour or two later).

If you find your milk supply dropping, there are several things you can do. Increase the number of feeds for a time (perhaps a week or so), until your supply builds up again. You can add a feed in the afternoon ("afternoon tea"), evening, and/or before one or more sleeps. Some mums find pumping after a feed, and storing the expressed milk into a bottle to give after the next breastfeed, helpful. Hopefully, all these things would be temporary to build up your supply again.

Make sure that you are drinking lots of water, and consuming enough calories to maintain your milk supply, as well as maintaining YOU. Exercise is great – but over-doing it may jeopardise your supply, so be wise with how much exercise you do.

*Introducing Solids*

Most nine month olds are happily gobbling up an increasing variety of food.

A few babies at nine months still have trouble swallowing, or don't seem interested in solid food. If

> **Try to avoid constant snacking – keep meals confined to high chair times.**

they are thriving on breastmilk, then they may just not be ready yet. Wait a week or two and try again – they will get the idea when they are ready. Almost all babies will start solids from around 6 months, but a small few are happy to wait longer to get started – even up until 12 months.

Try to avoid constant snacking – keep meals confined to high chair times. Occasional snacks, especially while out and about are fine. A plain biscuit or piece of fruit or cheese is a simple snack suggestion.

You can offer water in a sippy cup, especially just before naps.

There are many places available to find information about suitable food for babies of this age, but basically cereal and fruit for breakfast, vegetables/crackers and cheese/fruit/yoghurt for lunch, and vegetables (and maybe some meat) for dinner are common meals. Your Clinic Sister will help you here.

If you are breastfeeding and your baby doesn't want to eat much after his breastfeed, then don't panic! Most breast-fed babies are getting their main nutritional requirements from your milk, and so solid food is more of a bonus. If he is gaining weight and is well, then he may not need much extra food just yet. If he is struggling to gain weight, but is refusing solids after his breastfeed, you could try waiting 30-40 minutes after his breastfeed before offering some solids, to see if he becomes a little more interested in his food.

### *Highchair Manners*

High chair issues can become more difficult at this age. Screaming, back arching, food refusal (when they previously were happy to eat), throwing food or spoons etc. are all behaviours that commonly appear at around 9 months. Most of these behaviours can be associated with a lack of self-control. To avoid some of these problems you can teach him to hold the sides of the tray, or to keep his hands in his lap or flat on tray, during mealtime. My little Oliver was so good at this!

> **Mealtimes in our house are for eating.**

I don't allow my babies to feed themselves at this age – they just don't have the dexterity to do it effectively. Besides, once you give them the spoon to feed themselves with, it is mighty hard to take it back! Ask me how I know this ☺.

Some folks believe in allowing their babies to experience different textures through food. I disagree. If I wish my babies to experience different textures, I will use occasions apart from mealtimes to do that. Goop, playdough, water etc. are all fun, and when experienced in a controlled way, can be beneficial (providing they don't eat it!). Mealtimes in our house however, are for eating. I expect my older children to have good table manners. I would like to start going down that track, rather than have to go back and retrain later. A 9 month old is not going to have perfect table manners, nor understand why he would need to. However I can start with a few basic rules, like no playing in our food and throwing it around!

When babies of this age scream, arch, or throw things, we have always said in a stern, sad voice, "Oh dear. Back to your cot", and placed them in their cot for a few minutes until they are ready to come back and try again (with a "Good boy! Happy face!"), and without the tantrum. Usually a few minutes of isolation helps to get things under control, but sometimes they do persist. If you have tried it several times, but with no improvement, then perhaps it is time to finish up with mealtime.

Some families even start to teach their babies to use sign language from around 9 months onwards. Many babies don't spontaneously sign until a little later, but consistency will help them get it earlier. Usually a sign for 'please', 'thank you', 'more' and 'all done' are enough to get you started, and may help with some of those communication frustrations that they can have, especially in the high chair.

## Awaketime Activities

You can see by the sample routine, that the awaketimes are stretching longer at this age (so morning nap starts later). Meal times are also starting to stretch

> Try to have a balance between quiet and active play.

(no longer strict 4 hours – but moving towards lining up feeds with regular family mealtimes). If your baby is not quite ready to stretch one of his awaketimes yet, that's ok. Try again in a couple of weeks.

Stimulation during awaketime is good, but too much will unsettle his sleeps, so try to have a balance between quiet and active play.

The three main awaketime activities are **playing alone** (like playpen time), **playing near mum** (e.g. on floor while mum cooks or such – some families set up a 'play-centre'), and **playing with mummy** (singing, stories, etc.).

There will need to be a healthy balance between the three.

### Playpens

Playpen time twice a day is helpful – around 45-60 minutes after breakfast if possible, then 20-30 minutes in afternoon.

Between bath and dinner, or dinner and the last feed, is often a good time.

Provide a few toys and a book or two for him to play with, resisting the urge to constantly replace the toys during a playpen session. Too many toys at one time are a little overwhelming, so limit the number of toys in the playpen. Some babies, like my little Jemima, prefer a mixture of different toys (stacking cups, rattle, car, dolly etc). While others, like my little Elliot, prefer a small group of the same type of thing (container of little cars, blocks etc).

If this is your first go at playpen time, then start at 5 or 10 minutes and gradually increase that length of time.

It is not uncommon to hit a wall with babies at this age – your happy playpen baby is suddenly unhappy in the playpen! The world has suddenly become so very interesting to him, and he is bound to decide that he would prefer to be out there in it, rather than confined.

**Expensive toys are unnecessary.**

I have pushed on through this time – usually only a week or two, knowing that the benefits of playpen time make it worthwhile. It can help to shorten the playpen time (even to only 5 or 10 minutes if necessary). Follow it up with a cheerful "pack up time – good boy!" Using a tape or CD of music during this time can also help – he will quickly learn that the last song means it is time to pack up.

Expensive toys are unnecessary. Babies are quite happy with Tupperware, pegs, and other household items. Go ahead and let Grandma buy them expensive toys if she wishes, but don't feel that you need to spend a lot of money on entertaining your 9 month old.

### Managing Mobility

Once he becomes even more mobile, you will probably find that rotating activities, keeping a routine for the day, and avoiding too much 'roaming around' time is helpful to stop him getting into too much mischief. One or two short free roaming times in the day are probably enough for a baby this age.

If you have an early walker, then it is ok to gate off rooms to keep him confined while you cook dinner and such. Just because he CAN walk, doesn't mean he has to go wherever and whenever he wants to! He will get lots more opportunities to practice his walking as he gets bigger. For now, keeping him a little more restricted for most of his day is fine.

Even using the highchair for some play activities is fine for part of his awaketime (e.g. when you are cooking dinner) to keep him from wandering off or going into the kitchen when you are busy. You could pop him in the highchair with a toy or book, and bring him close so he can watch you.

Blanket Time is another tool that some mums use to train their little ones to play happily in a small area. This is useful if you need your baby to play quietly at church, soccer or somewhere else, without wandering off. Place a blanket on the floor, with baby in the middle, and a few toys. As he crawls out of the blanket space, say 'no' in a stern voice and place him back in the centre of the blanket. Repeat this a few times, and then leave it for another time. Start with 5 minutes, and gradually increase to 20 minutes (or however long you need). It is helpful to begin blanket training before your baby is walking!

## Sleeptime

> **Many nine month olds are still unable to make it through to bedtime without that cat-nap.**

*Catnaps*

At nine months, most babies are having two 1½ or 2 hour sleeps (morning and afternoon), and a possible cat-nap in the late afternoon. Many babies are still unable to make it through to bedtime without that cat-nap. This is a nap that used to be 2 hours, but will naturally and gradually shorten to 20 minutes, and then not at all (usually around 10 months).

Sometimes babies at this age wake during their sleeptime, whimper or cry out, but then go back to sleep with a little more fussing. This is fine. If they persist in fussing, you can go in and resettle, but then leave to allow them to go back to sleep again on their own.

### Sleep Tools

Patting is a common method parents use to put their babies back to sleep. It seems nice and easy when they are little babies, but it can become less fun if they depend on it in order to get back to sleep.

If you have been patting up to now, or have used another method that involves staying with your baby until he falls asleep, then now is a good time to rethink your getting-to-sleep methods. It will help to spend a few days working hard on this – probably those days when you are home rather than out and about or at work (it might be a tricky few days).

If baby has been having some trouble with sleeps, and needs to get back on track, it is time to try a Plan. It's ok to give him a yummy cuddle and good night kisses before sleep, but then pop him into bed and say "night-night". Leave the room and give him 5-10 minutes to try to settle. Then go in and lie him down with your calm voice saying, "No more play time. It's sleep time. Go to sleep", and leave the room. Try again every 15 minutes or so – same thing. The first few days, I would expect very little sleep, and much crying!

However, consistency is the key, and most parents see encouraging results in the first few days. By the end of the week, you should be feeling confident that things are getting back on track. You want him to learn to fall asleep on his own, or at least remain happily settled in his cot for a sleep time. This is a learned skill, and he will learn it if given the opportunity. The first time you give in, he will know that you will give in if he persists, so hang in there!

## Weaning

For many mums, there is no need to wean a baby at nine months. However some mums are wanting to wean now because they are going to work or wanting to plan to fall pregnant. Even illness, family upheaval or some other reason can mean that weaning is desirable. If your baby has been a great feeder up to now, then this can be a little traumatic – for mum as well as baby!

> **It is usually best to drop the feeds one at a time, to prevent engorgement and mastitis.**

Many mums find it easier to go straight to a sippy cup, rather than a bottle. At nine months, most babies are able to manage a sippy cup quite well. Formula is recommended until around 12 months.

It is usually best to drop the feeds one at a time to prevent engorgement and mastitis. The midday feed is often the easiest to drop first, followed (after a week or so) by the late afternoon feed. The last feed to go can be either the last night feed, or the first morning feed.

Some mums keep one or two breastfeeds for quite some time, and this can often work quite well. This might mean feeding in the morning and/or evening, while giving formula (or cow's milk if over 12 months) throughout the day. I managed to do this with several of my children for a few months before losing my milk (usually due to another baby coming!).

Of course you don't have to wean at nine months if you don't want to, and all is going well. The World Health Organization recommends feeding past 12 months. So if baby and your milk supply are healthy, continue to enjoy this special time of breastfeeding with your baby for a few (or many) months longer.

## Frequently Asked Questions...

**My 9 month old has started screaming in the high chair. I can't work out what she wants! How do I stop her screaming?**

This is one of those things that we have also had to deal with, and it is not fun!

It could be a communication problem. She may want to communicate something to you, but is unable to find a way apart from screaming. Or, she may be bored, tired or frustrated.

The quickest way to stop her from screaming will be to take her out of the high chair with a "no screaming", and pop her in her cot for a few minutes. Sometimes she might stop screaming in the cot, so you can bring her back to try again. Other times you might need to give her 5 or 10 minutes to calm down. Then you can try putting her back in the highchair, to see if she can be quiet. If not, then it's back to the cot with a "no screaming". Calm and consistent perseverance will get there in the end.

Some families also find that starting sign language training at this age can help with communication.

**I have been trying to teach my 9 month old how to sign for a few weeks now. She doesn't seem to be getting it yet. Shouldn't she be signing by now?**

While she may not look like she is getting it yet, it is probably all going in. Just keep making signing a natural part of the day.

So for example, when you hand her some food or a toy, sign and say "Thank you". Take hold of her hand and sign it for her while saying, "Thank you", followed by "Good girl!"

She is taking it all in, and one day she will do it spontaneously. Usually around the age of twelve months.

## My 9 month old is an early walker. He wants to go everywhere and get into everything, and I am exhausted trying to keep up with him. How am I going to entertain him all day?

There is no need to entertain your early walker all day! It would be helpful for you to divide his awaketime into different areas: play alone, play with mum, play near mum. This means that he might only be walking around for parts of his awaketime, rather than his whole awaketime.

He can spend some of his awaketime (twice a day) in his playpen. He can spend some of his awaketime in his high chair with some toys, or playing on a mat, or looking at books, or playing outside, or playing with you (or another member of the family). And for a part of his day, he can be allowed to potter around. Feel free to close off doors so that he isn't going to wander into a danger zone (bathroom, toilet, stairs etc) while you are not watching.

## My 9 month old has suddenly acquired separation anxiety! He won't go to anyone but me – even Grandma!

This is not an uncommon age for this problem to pop up. They are more aware of their surroundings at this age, and more understanding of relationships, so they often make some choices about to whom they want to go.

There are some things that you can do with his days that may prevent this behaviour from becoming a greater problem. Using the playpen twice a day will help, especially if it is more out of sight, rather than in full view of you. If he can see you throughout his playpen time, he will feel the need to be with you when he is given a choice. Move that playpen so that while you can check on him, he can't watch you the whole time.

Another thing that might help is to not give in to his demands for your attention every single time. If Grandma picks him up and he reaches for you, don't feel that you need to immediately 'rescue' him. This might only reinforce to him that you need to rescue him from Grandma. Try waving goodbye and leaving the room for a minute or to, to see if he will settle with Grandma. A few practice sessions of this type of thing should hopefully help him to relax with people other than you.

Remaining cheerful and consistent will see this phase through in a few weeks, so hang in there.

**When do we start dropping milk feeds with our 10 month old, and is it a problem if she is really keen on the bottles at the moment? She is on formula and having four to five bottles of 150 – 200ml each. We tried dropping the late 'dreamfeed' she has always had at about 10.00pm - 10.30pm, but she seems to either wake for it screaming or won't resettle herself in the early hours of the morning.**

Four to five feeds at this age are great.

You could try waking her for that last feed 15 minutes earlier each night, until she does no longer need it (much like dropping that last breastfeed).

You would be sure to offer her 200mls at each feed, so that you know she will not get less milk if she does drop that feed.

Usually, they can go to three or four milk feeds (plus meals and morning/afternoon tea) after around 12 months. Sometimes breastfed babies will keep four or five feeds past 12 months to maintain mum's milk supply for longer, but bottle fed babies will usually not need more than four or five feeds.

**My 10 month old baby has learned to stand and crawl around the cot. Until now, a sleeping bag has seemed to stop her doing this, but doesn't stop her any more. She keeps standing and screaming at the end of the cot, and is quite hard to resettle. Do we still leave her the 15 minutes crying and then go in and try and make her lie down?**

Getting stuck in the cot is a tricky problem at this age of newly-standing, and wanting to be more mobile. Fortunately it is usually fairly short lived.

Sometimes people find that it is easier to stop putting them in sleeping bags, so that they can get down from a standing position easier. Others find it easier to keep them in. Perhaps it is worth trying a few different things to see which works for you.

Leaving her to cry 15 minutes when you know that this is the problem is maybe too long in this case. I might try 5 minutes, then go in and lay her down, and say in a calm voice, "No, it's sleep time" (or something like that). I would expect her to continue trying to stand for a little longer, but she will eventually stop.

Sometimes they have trouble getting down. It can be helpful practicing getting down from a standing position during her playtime.

Hang in there! Hopefully this stage won't last too much longer!

**My 10 month old baby has stopped sleeping well during the day. He is teething, he has a cold, and we have been out and about quite a lot lately. Should I just let him cry for the rest of his sleep time?**

These times of sickness are frustrating and tiring for baby and mum.

They are also times when we might do something a little differently.

If he is waking during his sleep time and is snuffly and miserable, then letting him cry for another hour is not going to help. Try giving him 10-15 minutes to see if he will settle, and then go in and pick him up. This is a good time to listen to his cries and try to determine if he is crying in a trying-to-get-back-to-sleep way, or a I'm-not-going-back-to-sleep-today way.

If he is winding down, then it is usually best not to wake him up again by picking him up. If he is inconsolable, then a cuddle might be what is needed to help him relax enough to sleep. He may also take a few sips of water during this tough time of getting back to sleep.

If you are going out quite a lot, he will struggle even more, especially if he is already feeling unwell. Perhaps now is a time to stay home for a few days, and patiently allow him to recover, and get back on track with his normal sleep routine.

And sometimes during these days of sickness, we end up with an unhappy baby on our laps or in our arms for much of their sleeptime and awaketime.

Yes, it is tiring to be comforting a miserable baby who isn't sleeping well, but hopefully it will be short lived.

# Nine Month Baby Review
*After 9 Months reflect on how baby is going...*

## Weight and Growth
Weight:
Length:

## Feedtime
Duration(milk+solids):

20 mins or under □   20-40 mins □   40-60 mins □

Baby is usually feeding around

every 2 hrs or less □   2-3 hrs □   3+ hrs □

Baby is now eating...
Any concerns?

Other reflections on feeding...

*if bottle feeding* mls per feed:

## Sleeptime
Baby is going to bed:                                        awake □   asleep □

Duration of baby's sleep:
less than 60 mins □   60-90 mins □   90-120 mins □   120+ mins □

Resettling:                           most sleeps □   some sleeps □   rarely □

Baby's routine looks like...

Any concerns?

Other reflections on sleeping...

## Awaketime
during awaketime my baby is now...

**Mum reflections**

The best things about these 9 months have been...

The hardest things about these 9 months have been...

I am thankful to God for...

After 9 months I am feeling...

*Spread love wherever you go.*
*First of all in your own house be the living expression of God's kindness.*
*Mother Theresa*

*The Lord your God will always be at your side, and He will never abandon*
*you.*
*Deuteronomy 31:6*

# Chapter Seven

# Twelve month olds

Happy Birthday Baby!

Hasn't that first year flown by?

Now your baby is no longer a baby, but becoming a little person. Most are mobile – at least crawling or wriggling around on their bottoms, and quite a few are walking. Some are starting to talk, or at least making themselves understood. This all presents new challenges.

In this chapter we will consider some ideas of what your 12 month old might be up to in his routine, and have a little look at the next few months ahead.

A 12 month old often has a routine that fits in nicely with the rest of the family. It might look a little like this:

| | |
|---|---|
| 7:00 | wake, milk feed, breakfast, playpen etc. |
| 10:00 | nap |
| 12:00 | lunch (incl. milk), play etc |
| 3:00 - 5:00 | nap, afternoon tea drink/snack |
| 5:30 | bath and playpen |
| 6:00 | dinner (incl. milk) |
| 7:00 | final milk drink (if needed) |
| 7:30 | bed |

## Feedtime

### Family Mealtimes

At 12 months, most of baby's mealtimes will be close to lining up with regular family mealtimes.

> **At 12 months, most of baby's mealtimes will be close to lining up with regular family mealtimes.**

This means breakfast with the family (after a breast/bottle feed), lunch with the family, and then dinner. Sometimes it is still easier to give your 12 month old dinner earlier, then let him have playpen time or similar while the rest of the family eats.

Most of his meals at 12 months will be the same food that the rest of the family is eating. So regular healthy cereal, sandwiches, then meat/vegetables for dinner, plus fruit, cheese etc. Although most 12 month olds have teeth, you will probably need to cut up (or mash) his tougher food for a short while longer.

If you are breastfeeding then remember to **breastfeed first**, to maintain your supply.

*Fussy Eaters*

At this age, our cute little babies can begin to be quite demanding and opinionated about their food!

Now is a time to consider where you want to go with this. If you are going to give your toddler choices about food, then hang on for a rough ride! They can be very fickle – seeming to like something one day, detest it the next. How will you deal with this? Most of the time, these likes and dislikes are more about being in control than about taste.

In our family we always give our children a choice: this or nothing! It has been handy to start going down this track, instead of backtracking with an opinionated toddler. This means that for our family, I might give my 12 month old a Vegemite sandwich for lunch. If he ate it yesterday, but refuses it today, I do not go and make a different sandwich. He is either hungry, or not hungry!

This has been very helpful to us over the years, and now while my children have preferences, they do eat everything without an argument.

*Spoons, Fingerfood and Signing*

Another possible area of dispute is the spoon.

I am happy to give my toddlers finger foods for lunch and snacks, but I maintain the feeding of breakfast and dinner until they are old enough to manage a spoon without lots of mess or difficulty. This has come later for my children – somewhere between 15 and 24 months, depending on the child.

Teaching them to hold their hands down helps when trying to spoon feed. When giving sandwiches or snacks, I give them to baby one at a time, rather than a whole plate – it often gets dumped on the floor! If they only have one thing to focus on, they are more likely to eat than play.

If you have started using signing, then 12 months is an age where they will often start to 'get it'. Using signing in the high chair to indicate 'more', 'all done' 'thanks', and 'please', has been very handy, and reduced the frustrating whining that can build up.

*Highchair Tantrums*

What to do when tantrums arise in the highchair?

I have found (through much trial and error!) that isolation at the first sign of trouble is the quickest way to deal with toddler high chair tantrums. I will just pop them in their cot with an "Oh dear, back to your cot until you find your happy face." While some days we have had a few trips to the cot and back, mostly they learn rather quickly that they behave in the high chair or they leave.

*Snacks*

I also find that at this age, it is easier to give all morning/ afternoon tea snacks in the high chair, rather than allowing them to roam around the house with food. They are messy, and it helps teach them some self-control to be sitting in the high chair for all food and drink.

> **I do not believe in grazing all day.**

Which brings me to the issue of snacks. Some parents feel they need to give their 12 month olds snacks – morning and afternoon tea. If this fits with your routine, then that is fine. It's especially handy if out and about to have snacks on hand.

However, I do not believe in grazing all day. When toddlers learn to graze – eat whenever they desire – it increases problems with whining and tantrums. When I am able to say "Not now, wait till snack/meal time", they learn to be content and wait patiently until food time.

You may not need to give a morning tea snack until they drop that morning sleep at around 18 months or so, and just offer them a drink of water before their nap instead.

*Bottles*

Most 12 month olds are able to drink out of a sippy cup (rather than a bottle) for milk, watered-down juice or water. You might consider making that one-year birthday a time to start replacing the bottle with a cup. If baby is unwell, or you are on holidays or such, you may want to delay a little bit longer.

It is fine to offer water at times other than snack times. Juice is sweet and appropriate once a day or so (watered down), but it is not good for their teeth to have juice constantly available. Water is much more healthy.

If you have been using formula, then cow's milk (barring allergies, or family history of lactose intolerance) may be used from now on.

## Awaketime

A 12 month old will probably now be able to manage longer awaketimes.

*Planning the day's play*

Dividing his awaketimes into **time alone, time near mum,** and **time with mum** helps to break up his day and give him some consistency.

> **Watch out for wandering around and getting up to mischief!**

For **time alone,** the playpen is still handy twice a day. Rotate toys weekly to give variety. Watch the location – some babies have been happy to occupy themselves in the corner of the lounge room, but as they get older, the bustle of activity can be too distracting. They may need to be moved to another room or bedroom out of sight.

A baby can stick with playpen time until he is around the age of two. After that, you can replace the playpen with roomtime.

Another thing to watch out for – especially as he becomes more and more mobile, is how much time he has to wander around getting up to mischief. I have tried to minimise exploring time to particular times of the day, in order to cut down on conflict.

This has meant: getting him out of bed, changing nappy, and putting him straight in the high chair for breakfast after a breast/milk feed. Then after breakfast, I would take him straight to the playpen for 45-60 minutes or so. Then he can have some brief pottering around time until his nap soon after. After his nap, it's straight into the highchair for lunch and then some more play time.

In avoiding times in-between activities where they are just wandering around, my babies have avoided getting up to too much mischief.

**Time near mum** includes time where they might play in their high chair with blocks or books, or some other toy, while you are busy in the kitchen. Or perhaps on the floor with some plastic containers. Or perhaps in the pram with some toys while you hang out washing. They are playing but also interacting with mum from time to time.

**Time with mum** (and/or dad, siblings, friends, grandparents etc) is that special one on one time that we so enjoy with our babies! Singing, talking, dancing, reading, playing, doing puzzles are all fun things to do with our babies. With our first child, we will spend much of his awaketime time one-on-one with him, but as more children arrive, this time is divided up amongst siblings a little more. If you have several or many children, don't forget to spend some special playtime with your baby everyday!

### Sleeptime

> **12 month olds often do best on two day-sleeps each day.**

12 month olds often do best on two day-sleeps each day. Each sleep should be around 1½ or 2 hours long. They also will usually be able to sleep 10-12 hours at night.

*When one sleep turns into two sleeps*

Sometimes issues arise between twelve and fourteen months of age, when they seem to decide that they do not need two sleeps. They might sleep for the morning nap, but then refuse to go to sleep in the afternoon. Sometimes they cry and protest loudly, and other times they are quite happy – just not sleeping! Sometimes when they do finally go to sleep, it is at the end of the sleep time, so mum needs to decide whether to let them sleep or wake them up. If they sleep longer, then they struggle to go to sleep at bedtime. It can become a vicious cycle!

While it is a fairly common problem at this age, it is usually short lived. Many mums debate whether or not their baby is ready to drop a sleep, but most discover that he is tired and grouchy in the late afternoon.

What to do? I have found the best solution is to put him to bed as usual. If he cries, then I would go in from time to time and resettle – "Lie down, it's sleep time". I would get him up near the end of his usual sleep time, and carry on as usual.

Consistency here means that this phase usually lasts for just a few weeks. After that, they usually go back to sleeping their two naps again. Around the age of 18 months or so, they can go to one longer sleep after an early lunch.

Another question sometimes arises regarding baby waking up early in the morning or halfway through a nap, with a dirty nappy. Unfortunately there isn't often much that can be done about this, apart from changing him and putting him back to bed. Hopefully it won't last forever, and they will soon sleep through without the need for a nappy change.

Sometimes these problems can feel like they are going on forever, when it is only a few weeks or months in the life of your child!

## Frequently Asked Questions...

**Any tips for what we do to adjust our 12 month old to our time when daylight saving comes? She's waking at the crack of dawn already!**

Basically, it may happen gradually. Try stretching her 15 minutes a day or so, until she is happy with the new time.

It will sort itself out in a couple of weeks. Be prepared for a couple of transition weeks, and half the worry is gone.

**When returning home from an outing (after no sleep), what strategies can I use to calm him back down enough to get him to sleep because he's so overtired?**

If baby is so overtired that he can't calm down to sleep after being out, then some quiet cuddling, rocking, singing etc may be needed. Depending on his age, and what his routine is like, a breastfeed or at least a cup/bottle of water offered, can be also something that helps him settle. As long as it is not happening everyday, then this time of resettling is fine. Keep it calm, quiet, in his room. As he starts to get heavy, and his eyes are trying to close, pop him into bed for his nap.

If you are frequently out and about, and this is a daily problem, then a rethink of your activities might also be helpful. While mums sometimes struggle to stay home, babies prefer it!

**My 12 month old is on a bottle. When do I wean him to a cup, and how do I do that?**

Most 12 month olds are quite capable of moving to a sippy cup from a bottle.

The advantages to changing now are that he will quickly get used to a cup and forget the bottle, and it is much easier to clean.

The longer baby continues with a bottle, the more attached to it he becomes, making it harder to wean onto a cup. The bottle can be used more for comfort than drink, leading to bottles being carried around the house and left in beds. This has been shown to contribute to tooth decay, as baby goes to sleep with sugary drink in his mouth.

So how to wean? Basically similar to weaning from the breast – one feed at a time. Start with lunch, then afternoon/ dinner, and leaving morning or last feed to last. Just give baby milk in his sippy cup in the highchair with his meal. Keep bottles out of sight if baby is particularly attached to them.

Try to avoid routines that will leave him wanting his bottle like putting him to bed with a bottle. If you want him on the cup, then best to avoid temptation to think of the bottle!

Once he has gone without bottle for a day or two, then matter-of-factly refuse any mention of it. The desire for bottle will most likely pass quicker for baby than for mum!

**My 12 month old is still having two breastfeeds a day (morning and night), but I want to wean her, in order to boost my fertility so that I can conceive our next baby. She is very attached to these feeds – how do I wean her?**

Well done on feeding for 12 months ☺.

Weaning your baby so that you can concentrate on regaining fertility is going to take some determination on your part. Do you want to wean, or would you rather breastfeed?

If you want to wean, then I suggest dropping one of your feeds, and replacing it with a sippy cup of milk (possibly given to baby by dad). After a week or so, you can drop the next feed.

Perhaps she has always associated the milk with a comfortable cuddle and breastfeed. Then it can help to only offer a sippy cup of milk in the high chair, with meals (breakfast or dinner). Perhaps Dad can help out with giving her these cups of milk if he is around.

Once you have moved to a sippy cup, then she should quickly get used to the idea – probably more quickly than mum!

## My nearly 13 month old is getting into stuff all day! How do I teach her not to touch those 'off limit' things – like the heater?

Your 13 month old is a smart little thing. She will easily learn what her boundaries are, if she knows that you are prepared to enforce them.

Some people try distracting their little one, or removing (or blocking) the forbidden object. This teaches them that anything they can touch is fair game!

We have found that it is quicker, easier and safer to teach them boundaries rather than remove all temptation. Some things of course we removed (precious or dangerous items), just not everything.

In our family it meant that when our little ones were heading towards a forbidden object (like the heater), we would start by saying "No" in a firm voice. If baby persisted, we would swat the back of their hand. Just hard enough to catch their attention, but not hard enough to really hurt. This gave them an immediate consequence for their choice to touch something that was off limits. We might repeat once if they are persistent, and then remove them to halt a power struggle.

Most of our little ones learnt fairly quickly that "No" meant to stop! Some learnt quicker than others, and some were rather stubborn. However learning this lesson at home meant that when we went visiting, we could be confident that our little ones had a sense of boundaries, and would respond to our verbal warning to stop what they were doing.

We also tried to plan their day so that they didn't have large amounts of roaming-around-the-house time. This always leads to trouble, as they are rather curious at this age, and enjoy finding interesting things to do when you are not watching them!

# Twelve Month Baby Review
*After 12 Months reflect on how baby is going...*

## Weight and Growth
Weight:
Length:

## Feedtime
Duration(milk+solids):

20 mins or under ☐  20-40 mins ☐  40-60 mins ☐

Baby is usually feeding around

every 2 hrs or less ☐  2-3 hrs ☐  3+ hrs ☐

Baby is now eating...
Any concerns?

Other reflections on feeding...

*if bottle feeding* mls per feed:

## Sleeptime
Baby is going to bed:                          awake ☐  asleep ☐

Duration of baby's sleep:
less than 60 mins ☐  60-90 mins ☐  90-120 mins ☐  120+ mins ☐

Resettling:                  most sleeps ☐  some sleeps ☐  rarely ☐

Baby's routine looks like...

Any concerns?

Other reflections on sleeping...

## Awaketime
during awaketime my baby is now...

**Mum reflections**

The best things about these 12 months have been...

The hardest things about these 12 months have been...

I am thankful to God for...

After 12 months I am feeling...

*The mother's heart is the child's classroom.*
*Henry Ward Beecher*

*A cheerful heart brings a smile to your face.*
*Proverbs 15:13*

# Chapter Eight

# 12-18 Months
## The next few months

> **The wheels have fallen off!**

Where are you going with your baby during the next few months?

For many families, once they reach 12 months of age those rapid routine changes slow down. For the next 6 months or so (until the dropping of that morning sleep), much of your baby's day might remain fairly constant.

The biggest battles however, will come with issues of control. Who will be in charge of your toddler's life? You? Or them?

I frequently get questions at around the 14 month mark: "The wheels have fallen off!"

Very often this is a case of baby gradually taking over the control of his days. This can happen without us even noticing…

He wants certain foods. He wants to do certain activities and he wants to go places. He gets tired, but not put down for regular naps. He gets up before he's had enough sleep. He is out and about too often, and can't cope. He likes things done in a particular way. His way!

While it is certainly appropriate to listen to him and consider his wants from time to time, when a pattern is established whereby he is always calling the shots – there will be trouble!

In these next few months consider where you are going with your baby, and who is going to lead the way.

**Where are you going with your baby, and who is going to lead the way?**

Having said that, they are delightful at this age – full of curiosity and learning. Enjoy him!

While you are enjoying him, consider training him…

... in **self-control** (gaining control over some of his impulses to outburst);

... in **obedience** (responding to your call, and following simple commands);

... in **patience** (waiting);

... in **contentment** (being thankful);

... and in **responsibility** ('helping').

Start to look at ways to teach these things now, within a flexible routine to your day. This will greatly help in those months (and years) to come - when he becomes very vocal, and even more opinionated! It will help to produce toddlers who really are terrific to be around.

I am including quite a few questions and answers from my inbox. Hopefully there will be some examples that you might find helpful in the coming months. Thank you to all those mums (and dads) who have asked interesting questions and given such great feedback on the subsequent results!

**Frequently Asked Questions...**

**Can you give some ideas for my 13 mth old's day?**

A 13-14 mth old's day might look like this...

- up and breakfast (milk, then solids in high chair)
- playpen time for 45-60 mins
- some free playtime
- bed for morning sleep (around 1.5-2 hrs)
- lunch (milk, then solids in high chair)
- some free play time
- outside time
- highchair time
- book time
- sleep time (around 1.5 - 2 hrs)
- free play time
- outside time
- bath time
- playpen time (20-30 mins)
- dinner  (milk, then solids in high chair)
- play with dad
- milk feed, then bed

**My 13 month old has started screaming when he doesn't get his own way. He is throwing things down and throwing himself on the floor - I am worried he will injure himself. We are trying not to give in to his tantrums, and just ignore him, but it doesn't appear to be working.**

There may be several things happening here.

Make sure he is having good sleeps. A tired toddler protests frequently- about everything!

Also, make sure he is getting enough fluids. Sometimes they aren't getting enough water to drink and get thirsty and cranky, but can't articulate that need. I suggest keeping all drinks to high chair in sippy cup (or at least sit him down). Avoid allowing him to wander around with a drink/bottle all day.

Check that his routine is quite tight. A toddler with too much free and roaming time will easily become difficult.

Another thing to check is that you are not asking him questions all day: Would you like a drink? Would you like this toy? Do you want to play outside? Do you want to get up? etc etc. This is highly confusing for a toddler and leads to them feeling like they must make a multitude of decisions all day. I suggest listening to yourself to see if you have fallen into this very common trap. If so, try turning your 'questions' into statements: You may have a drink now. You can play with this toy. It's outside time now. I will pick you up soon.

Of course you may respond to their requests if they are 'asking' for something, and you think it ok to give them what they ask. This is more about your own tone of voice, and the habit of asking them questions constantly.

I would try not to always fall into the 'let's see what he wants' game. We never win! You can decide what is best for him, and make those decisions (for now). If he is not happy with your decision, then removing him to his cot for a few minutes is the quickest way to curtail those tantrums (believe me - we have been through this more times than I can count, and it is the QUICKEST way to solve this one!!).

So for example, if he is in the high chair, and starts throwing food, arching, whinging etc, then straight away say "Oh dear, let's go to your cot and find your happy face" (or something like that). Give him a few minutes to see if he will settle down. If he starts to settle, you need to bring him straight back to the same situation (don't then give into him), and try again. We have had stubborn little ones go back quite a few times before settling down - especially when we first start working on it. Act decisively, and firmly but calmly as soon as he starts to exert himself. This will help get things under control before he (and you!) really loses the plot :)

## I haven't done playpen or roomtime with my 14 month old. Is it too late to start? How can I introduce it now?

Playpen time is always going to be easier if it is started early, but it is not too late. It will take longer, and a little bit more effort, though!

I would start with 5 minutes morning and night. Yes, she will probably protest for the first week or 2! Remember to cheerfully say "playpen time is over" at the end of the 5 minutes, regardless of how she has managed (or not!).

Once she starts to show signs of 'enjoying' the time, or at least settling for a minute or 2 to play with her toys, you can begin to extend that time a little. It will take some time, some encouragement, and consistency. I do think however, that it is possible.

**My 14 mth old falls asleep on the floor, but when I move him to his cot he wakes up and just screams for the rest of sleeptime. How can I get him to sleep in the cot for his day sleep?**

It sounds like you may have allowed him to fall into a pattern of falling asleep before he has been put to bed. It will help to work on putting him to bed before he falls asleep, rather than allowing to fall asleep away from his cot. I imagine he would not be happy about this. If he is used to falling asleep elsewhere, it will take some determination on your part.

I would suggest giving him some water in a sippy cup before bed (if he doesn't otherwise drink before bed), and then laying him down with a firm (but kind!) "it's time for sleep now". He will most likely protest loudly. I would give him 10-15 minutes before going in each time to lay him down again and calmly tell him that it is sleep time.

After an hour (or possibly longer if you are up to it) of this, I would get him up. Day 1!

You would need to make sure that EVERY sleep he is put down in his bed awake (rather than letting him fall asleep anywhere), at least until this bad patch is over. He is old enough to meet your resolve, so you would need to be consistent with this for a whole week. Hopefully after a few days you will see him start to give up during his naptime, and fall asleep on his own. Yippee! That is what you are working towards.

Am I making sense here?

There are no magic solutions, only a few days of determination on your part to crack these habits. As long as there are no other underlying problems (medical, food issues, major trauma at home etc), then I am sure he can be re-trained to go to sleep in his crib.

**My baby is now 14 months. Sometimes he seems to want two sleeps, but he is often only sleeping for one sleep. But he is so unhappy! Also, he is throwing his blanket out of the cot. What do I do??**

Oh dear! Those 14 month blues!

It is really common to have difficult day sleeps at around this age. I always just put them to bed for the normal time. If they sleep, great. If not? Oh well, they get up at the right time (sometimes a little earlier if they have been persistent in their protests) and move on. Usually quite grumpily until they give in and resume having two sleeps a day. Which they usually do eventually – so hang in there! Oh, I do go in every so often to check on them if they are unhappy ☺.

This is a time to watch some things during the day. Keep a tight routine for activities. The more free roaming time, the more sleep time battles. Make sure you are being consistent with instruction and discipline: "no, don't touch", "Come to Mummy". Try not always giving in to his demands (wanting a drink/food/toy etc) so that he feels like he is always in charge. If he thinks he is in charge of everything during the day, he will be more likely to be difficult at sleep time (when you are making him do something he doesn't want to do).

You can use your calm voice when going in to resettle him ("You must lie down, it is sleep time"), and try to avoid picking up his blanket every time it is dropped. It is possibly only a test for you to see how long until you come in and pick it up!

**My little one is now 15 months. We have had lots of disruptions in our household, and the wheels have fallen off! We have lost our routine, our day sleeps, and our happy baby – where do we start to get him back?**

The first thing to do is sit down and write out a plan for the day. Something to aim for. Here is a suggestion for a 15/16 month old – feel free to alter times and such to suit your own home.

- 7.00am – up and breakfast.

Breastfeed with mummy (if still breastfeeding), then to the highchair for breakfast. I recommend putting him straight into the highchair from bed, and straight into the playpen from high chair. Reduces any opportunities for mischief!

- Then playpen time.

Somewhere where he won't be distracted by activity. Starting with 5 minutes, and working up to 45-60 minutes as he plays happily. Use your happy voice, regardless of his protests: "It's playpen time! Good Boy!" and "Playpen time is over! Good Boy!"

- Then some morning activities.

Outside time, books, free floor play. You can work out the order that suits your family.

- Morning nap.

Perhaps try 10.30 or 11 through till around 12. He may not be happy, but persistence will pay off! Try giving him a drink of water before putting him to bed.

- 12/12.30 – lunch

- If he has had a nap in the morning, then he can now have some playtime – outside, books, floor play before his next nap at around 2 - 4.

- If he didn't nap in the morning (because he protesteth too much, or you were out and about etc), then pop him to bed after lunch (12.30 until around 3/3.30). Some stories, a drink and a cuddle, then bed.

- After his afternoon nap (finishing around 3-4), he can have a snack, and some floor play.

- Bath at 5.00, followed by more playpen time while you finish cooking dinner.

- Dinner at around 6, followed by snuggles, story and bed around 7-7.30.

You will need to be consistent with teaching him to obey your instructions during the day. "Don't touch!" or "Oh dear, we don't throw tantrums, off we go to your cot to find your happy face" and other things like that. You can't expect him to stay in bed, if he is in control of all his activities during the day!

### At what age should we transition our 15 mth old from the cot to a big bed?

Unless you have a new baby brother or sister needing that cot, then you may consider keeping your toddler in a cot for a little bit longer. Once they have a taste of the freedom to hop in and out of bed, it can be a hard thing to rein in again. Ours usually stayed in the cot until they were around 22 months, and their cot was needed for their younger sibling. Some babies stay in their cots until past the age of 2. And some babies do move to the big bed under 18 mths, although it does mean more training to help them stay put.

When you do decide to transition, you can try starting with day sleeps in the bed, while nights stay in the cot, until he has got the hang of things. This allows you to be around to help him remember to stay on his bed during rest time.

### Can you give me an idea of what my 16 mth old might be doing during the day - especially now she is down to one sleep?

Here is a sample routine for a toddler age around 16/18 months:

- breakfast: breast/solids.

I pick them up from bed and pop them straight in the high chair, especially if they have trouble with running around the house and creating havoc before breakfast!

- playpen.

Around 30-60 minutes depending on how well they are coping. If you are just starting or just getting back into playpen time and she is struggling, try to stay out of her sight. Start with 5 minutes, just a few toys, and a cheerful "all done!" when the time is up. Even using a timer or taped music can be helpful.

- focus play.

Some time with mum/dad - books, puzzles, toys

- outside time.

A walk or play in in the yard

- lunch: breast/solids

- rest time.

Read a story first, then bed for 2-3 hours (hopefully!)

- up, drink/snack and free play

- outside play

- bathtime

- focused play time.

Use the playpen, bedroom or even table time - while watching dinner prep in high chair with toy or book

- dinner (solids)

- quiet play and breastfeed

- bed.

**My 16 mth old is happy in playpen time. Is she ready to go to roomtime now?**

It is probably a little too early to move to roomtime just yet. That great big bedroom may not look big to you, but it is a giant playpen to a 16 mth old. There will probably be places in there that she is not old enough to manage well (like unpacking drawers, pulling out baby wipes, or playing in nappy rash cream!). A playpen is still a useful play space until the age of around 2.

**My 17 mth old has suddenly decided not to eat very much at all. I am worried that he is not getting enough food, but he simply refuses everything I offer him - even the things he used to love! How can I get him to eat again?**

It is really very common to notice a decrease in food consumption at this age. Try not to stress over it. Unless he is unwell or demonstrating other unusual and worrying behaviours, he is most likely just not needing as much to eat right now.

We always gave a choice when offering food - this or nothing! If he has eaten a particular food before and suddenly refuses it, it is more likely not an issue of taste, but a desire to play the 'food game', or simply a lack of hunger. He will eat when he is hungry, and he will survive the days he doesn't seem to eat much. Keep food to structured mealtimes (rather than trying to feed him in between meals), and in the high chair (rather than running after him and offering him food). And make sure he has plenty of opportunities to drink water through the day.

**My 17 mth old is waking up early every morning. 5-5.30 is too early to get up, but he is screaming every day until we go and get him. He is such a good boy all through day - almost no issues at all - except for his very short day nap. How can I help him stay in bed a little longer in the mornings?**

I wonder if he would benefit from a tighter day routine, which includes a longer sleep time. If he wakes too early for you, you can try letting him know that it is not time to get up yet, and to have 'quiet time' until getting up time.

Sometimes these rather compliant ones seem to coast through their days, but hit a wall at some point (usually bedtime, mealtime or wakeup time). This is often because they tend to get through their days with very minimal correction - they seem to be doing all they are required from mum. This can be because they have become experts in keeping things flowing smoothly, while still thinking in their own heads that they are actually in charge of their days. Because they often don't make much of a fuss, and mum tends to go along with what they want so that conflict is reduced, they can become very disagreeable when they hit that wall of I-will-do-what-I-want-in-this-area! For some, this may be afternoon rest time and/or morning wakeup time.

If this sounds like it may be what is happening in your house (and it is quite common!), then the solution will involve a bit of hard work on your part. You will need to tighten up all his day activities, so that you are telling him what activities are next, and how long he can do each activity. If he has become used to quietly running the show, you would expect major problems within the first few hours, as he realises that he is no longer in charge of his day! If you do decide to change a few things and take charge of his day, you will need to plan ahead. You'll want to be able to stick to your plan without giving in to him. Avoid saying "ok, you can stop that activity now since you are having a fit", or "ok, mummy won't make you do such-and-such since you don't want to"!

Problems like short day naps, and early mornings usually become less frequent, when people start to make these changes. It does take time, though - at least a week or 2 if you are consistent.

Working on his playpen time will help too. Try starting with around 15-30 minutes and gradually increase it up to around 60 mins. If he becomes upset before pack up time, cheerfully encourage him to wait it out for a few more minutes.

Write out an achievable day routine. Try to balance it with activities where he is playing alone (eg playpen, roomtime, outside time, video time), playing near to you, but not 'with' you (like play dough, cars on the floor, colouring, blocks etc), and time when you are playing together (eg reading books, doing puzzles together etc).

**My toddler is 17 mths, and we are soon to have our second baby. Can you give me some tips on preparing her for the birth of a sibling? I have been reading her books on new babies, but she doesn't seem to understand.**

Congratulations on the next baby - what fun! My first 5 were 19-21 months apart, so I can relate to your questions. You are quite right. At this age, they have no understanding of what is going to happen in the family. They can pat the 'baby' bump and such, but they really have NO idea. I think those preparation books are probably more suitable for older children (2-3+ years).

However, I never found the new baby caused any problems at all! They are so young at that age, that they soon forget there was any other world than that with baby. I did use the term 'mummy's baby' to make sure they understood that the new baby wasn't for them to play with yet. A dolly which can be 'her baby' can help that a little. Basically, I think that since the beginning of time, young siblings have been able to handle a new baby without all the psycho-babble that we worry ourselves about!

## Can you give me some ideas for going from 2 sleeps to 1 sleep with my 18 mth old?

It doesn't usually happen overnight. You may find that you alternate for a while until it happens every day.

When moving to one sleep, I give them an early lunch (around 11.30), followed by bed. They are usually rather tired by the end of the morning. Sometimes they go straight to a 3 hour sleep (which is wonderful!), but sometimes they have shorter sleeps and wake up grumpy. This might mean that you need to work on keeping her in bed to sleep for a little longer.

Decide on your bedtime routine - drink, story, kiss and cuddle etc - and then try to be consistent with each nap or bed time.

## My 18 mth old is really struggling with going to sleep at night. She wants everything done in a particular way, in a particular order. She is screaming and fighting with us, and we are exhausted trying to get her to sleep. And then she is waking again in the middle of the night and screaming again - and so we start up the whole long process again. She is only sleeping for an hour or so in the afternoon, so she MUST be tired! Help!

It is quite common for little ones around this age (and onwards) to choose a battle that they are prepared to fight to the end.

For some it is mealtime. Or bath time. Or afternoon nap time. Or change time.

It seem like for you right now, it is bedtime. It seems like SHE has decided that she will only co-operate at bed time if she has her little world they way she wants it. Unless there is something else happening that I am not aware of, I suspect this is a tantrum- and the symptom of a problem! The longer you continue to 'give in', the longer it will take to resolve. However, as you have discovered, it is extremely distressing!!

So what might the actual problem be? Sometimes it starts out after a previously distressing experience (like a bad storm etc). Sometimes it is just a pattern that has built up over time.

More likely, is that in her little head, she thinks that these big decisions of her day are her own responsibility (not yours). So, when she thinks you are calling the shots (instead of her), she will communicate loud and clear that deviations from her rules will not be allowed.

If this is what the actual problem is, then what to do?

Firstly, I would have a look at what is happening during the day.

It is rather easy to get into a pattern of allowing them to make lots (and lots) of little decisions throughout the day. Even when we don't mean to. It can happen when we continually ask them what they'd like to do next.

Would you like a drink? Would you like to sit down over here? Would you like a bath? Would you like some dinner? Would you like a biscuit? Would you like to go to bed now?

Simply by phrasing our words into a question, we communicate that this is a decision that she is making (even if you know she really isn't). It is often those fairly compliant ones that cause these super battles - they seem to so happy through the day, and so compliant. But often this masks their tendency to feel in control of every situation. Then, when we are actually requiring them to do something they don't want to do, they kick up a (big) stink!

So I would start by listening to yourself through the day. Are you giving her lots of little choices about what she is doing? Have you noticed your voice inflection going up at the end of your sentences? If you notice that this is happening in your house - voila! A possible problem in the making!

But what to do next? If you change the way you are speaking and start to tell her, rather than ask her, what she is doing, then you should see a number of tantrums pop up. You should think to yourself: hmm, that's unusual for her to respond like that! This is good! If you can start to deal with that during the day (with those little things), you will have a better chance of managing her at bedtime. You have declared your authority in the little things of the day, and so at this big bedtime thing, you are reinforcing that you are still the boss.

So then at bedtime, you would need to be firm with her about what is going to happen. And then stick to your guns, with hubby backing you up if possible! You love her (you have shown her that all day), you will give her a hug and kiss goodnight, but you are still the boss!

I might consider giving her her milk before she goes into her room. Once she has had her milk, change, cuddle - whatever, you can pop her into bed. Whereupon she may just scream her head off!! After 10 minutes, you can go in and calmly reassure her that she is fine, but it is now bedtime. Repeat every 15 minutes! Expect the first night to last a couple of hours. Expect each subsequent night to take an increasingly shorter time.

Down the track, you will be able to have more opportunities to give her more choices during the day. But for now, I would take the reins on that one.

**My 18 mth old son is aggressive to me and to other toddlers. It is embarrassing at playgroup when he lashes out at the other children. What can I do to stop it?**

Try keeping him by your side, and holding his hand for the first little while at playgroup, until he relaxes enough to be able to totter off and play without feeling aggressive.

A child at this age is unlikely to play with another child in a fair way. They are more loners at this age - playing next to each other rather than with each other.

This can be tricky if an older child (like a 3 year old) wants to play with an 18 month old. While some children (especially extroverts, or the 2nd, 3rd or subsequent children in a family) can tolerate this, many oldest or only children, or introverts, really struggle. They will lash out at the other child because they just don't know how to manage the situation. Once he is around 2 1/2 - 3, you can start to talk through situations with him and role play, so that he can be better prepared and have better coping skills. But probably not so much now - he is probably a little too young.

I would also work harder on his aggression towards you at home. At 18 months his consequences need to be significant enough to be memorable. A "no!", a trip to his cot, or even a swat on the hand can help him see the seriousness of his ways.

I would also watch out for signs before he starts to get aggressive so you can intervene a little earlier. Watch for frustration, tiredness, hunger and anger. When you start to see signs of frustration, work on stopping and folding his hands to get self control. If you have a 'hot head', you may need to do this quite often! And they may not respond very compliantly! Still, it is worth working on now, while he is little.

**My baby is 18 mths and I am still breastfeeding all day and night. I want to wean him, but he is refusing to stop! He demands to be breastfed constantly- more for comfort than actual food, as he is eating and drinking all day - and won't fall asleep unless he is 'attached'. How am I going to wean him?**

It is going to be hard work, and entirely dependent on your resolve. Do you really want to wean at this age? Then you will need to stop offering the breast for comfort.

I would suggest that you set some short term goals. Perhaps you could only offer breast before meals (not during the night, or at bedtime). Then after a week or so, cut that down to one meal, then none at all.

Gradual weaning and being firm in saying no to a demanding toddler, is going to make it happen faster. Think too about having a tighter routine to your day, and consider other areas in his day where he is demanding. Sometimes it is part of a whole pattern of behaviour. It will be very tough for you both for a week or 2, but hang in there!

Of course, if you are happy to breastfeed for a while longer, you can do that too. In fact you could spend several months gradually weaning. It is entirely up to you.

**I have a 16 mth old and 3 yr old, and a new baby on the way. Where am I going to put the new baby? I don't want to put the baby in with the older two in case the baby wakes them up. Suggestions?**

Once we have more than one child, we kept our newborn babies in a large cane basket which could be moved around to different places depending on the time of day. During the day, they slept in our bedroom. During the night they usually in the next room ( on the dining table!). Once they were sleeping through the night, I was able to shift them back into the main kids' bedroom at night.

We also kept a port-a-cot in our room, which was handy as they got bigger and still needed to be able to sleep in their own space during the day. Our last baby spent nights in our room too because of space, so that is another option.

Chapter Nine  # Breastfeeding
## Tips for a New Mum

Before we have our first baby, breastfeeding looks and sounds so easy. We watch our friends feed their babies, we see pictures of smiling mothers and their fat, happy babies, and we wonder: how hard could it be?

> **Breastfeeding, once it is established, is a wonderful experience.**

And then we try it out! And we discover that it isn't always as easy at it looks.

Some mothers are blessed with stacks of rich milk that could feed a whole suburb. Some mothers struggle to even establish a milk supply, let alone continue feeding for months. Most mothers fall somewhere in-between. However, it is a learned skill – both for mum and baby. And often tricky for everyone to get going, and to keep going.

There is no doubt that breastfeeding is the healthiest option for our babies. In times past, it was the only option. With our busy lifestyles, our desire for our lives to be perfect, our paranoia about the psychological health of our babies, the pressure to go back to work, the horror stories of our friends and family, and the images of skinny mothers around us- it is a struggle before we even start!

Once it is established, breastfeeding is a wonderful experience. It is convenient (no bottles or formula to take with you), and it is a relaxing, snuggling time with your baby.

For mothers who despite all their efforts end up bottle-feeding, there can be a tremendous guilt placed on them by other, successfully breastfeeding mothers. It is not helpful for a breastfeeding mother to make a bottle-feeding mother feel any more guilty than she already is! Her baby will still grow up to be happy and healthy.

I have breastfed all six of my children. It was not always easy and I hope in this section to pass on those tips that I learned, and that helped things to go much more smoothly. Of course I can't cover everything here, and other mums may prefer to do things differently. But this is what I did. My children are all very healthy, and most of them were happily breastfed for past a year. Some of them did not want any solids until they were close to 12 months old.

In this chapter on breastfeeding, we will look at the following topics:

> **Looking after YOU**
>
> **The Mechanics of Feeding**
>
> **Feeding Routines**
>
> **Breastfeeding for the Long Haul**
>
> **Extra Bits**

## Looking after YOU

> **If you skimp on calories while you are trying to breastfeed, you may find that your baby is just not getting enough milk.**

*Eat, Drink and be Merry!*

And you thought you were hungry when you were pregnant!

Breastfeeding mums are notoriously hungry, and with good reason. You need to consume enough calories to feed your baby and keep you healthy. If you skimp on calories while you are trying to breastfeed, you may find that your baby is just not getting enough milk. Or that your body suffers while your baby grows fat. This early time of establishing your milk supply is not the time to diet, especially if you are struggling to get that supply going.

On the other hand, it is a time to be wise about eating, and not consume junk food in an effort to appease hunger pains. You need a healthy balance of protein (meat, fish, nuts, eggs), carbohydrates (breads, pasta, rice) and lots of fruit and veggies.

Likewise, you should be drinking plenty of water during this time of breastfeeding. A full glass of water at every feed is a good place to start.

Milk laden with a supplement (like Sustagen) is another helpful way to boost a slowing milk supply, especially if you have been unwell and need to get your body working efficiently again.

> It is so important for breastfeeding mothers to get adequate rest.

Sometimes the food that mum eats can cause discomfort to her feeding baby. Foods that are spicy or high in acid are common culprits for unsettled babies.

### Exercise: When and What

Some mums love to exercise regularly. This is usually fine, within reason. Jogging every day and going to the gym three times a week is probably not going to help your milk supply! A walk (or swim) each day, though, is fine and healthy.

### Afternoon Rests – Essential for New Mummies

It is so important for breastfeeding mothers (of any age baby) to get adequate rest. A lie down in the afternoon when baby is asleep is crucial throughout the whole period of breastfeeding, to help mum's body have a break.

Going to bed at a reasonable hour is also essential. Once baby goes down for the night, so does mum! No pottering around doing housework at midnight, or you will soon be exhausted as you try to keep up.

## Time for Mum

Make sure that you have some time in your week, or even each day, that is yours. You may love to read, knit, sew, stamp, scrapbook or enjoy some other hobby. Being a mum doesn't mean that you no longer get to enjoy doing those things you love to do. Allow yourself an hour or so each day, or a couple of times a week, to indulge in your hobby.

## Avoiding Mastitis and Sore Nipples

Mastitis is a nasty infection that affects the milk ducts. It often starts with blocked ducts – when the milk gets 'stuck' in the ducts. This can be identified by a 'hot spot' on the breast – redness and aching. Massaging that spot while feeding is very helpful in draining those ducts. You can also try using hot packs and warm showers.

If mastitis sets in, then you might feel 'fluey' – aching joints, fever, breast pain, and sore nipples. Drink lots of extra water! If things don't settle down in 12-24 hours, then it is important to see a doctor for some antibiotics to get rid of the infection.

In extreme cases, some mums need surgery to drain ducts, so it is worth taking seriously.

Sore nipples can also be excruciating. They can bleed even to the point of baby drinking, and then throwing up blood. They can be painful enough to make your toes curl up in pain! Yes, I do remember...!!

While many cases of sore nipples can be due to poor positioning, it does also seem that some mothers are prone to it regardless of their positioning. The good news is that they do toughen up in time, and that there are some creams available that help ease the pain and heal the sores. I found Lansinoh (a lanolin cream) helped, but there are others available (check with your doctor, midwife or pharmacist). Time also helps, so hang in there!

While breastfeeding can be painful when you have sore nipples or mastitis, it is very important not to stop breastfeeding. Push on, knowing that it is temporary and should soon pass.

## The Mechanics of Feeding

*Correct Attachment*

My first child Madeline, refused to latch on at all. She screamed and arched her back every time I tried for the first five days of her life. By day five, she had not had a single breastfeed! The nurses tried everything they could to make her feed. I was very sore after a difficult delivery, and I still am not sure how I kept sane during that first week! She eventually agreed to breastfeed with the aid of nipple shields, which I used for ten weeks.

> **For many mothers, that six week mark is a turning point, and things start looking up.**

The key here was persistence. I always advise struggling mothers to persist for six weeks if they can. For many mothers, that six week mark is a turning point and things start looking up.

It so important to start good habits. So for those first few days it is important to sit correctly. This means sitting with your hips back in the chair, your back straight, and your feet elevated a little, so that baby doesn't slide off your lap. If you hunch over your baby, it will be uncomfortable and tricky for baby to stay on correctly.

You will need pillows on your lap during the first weeks (especially if you have had a caesarian), to keep baby up high enough to feed comfortably. You won't need those pillows forever (unless you are nursing twins), but these first few days and weeks are important, when they are so little.

Always make sure that his chest and head are in line and facing towards your own chest. If his head is twisted, he will struggle to feed. His mouth needs to be open wide enough to cover most of the areola (the whole nipple area). If he is hungry, he should start sucking with gusto. At first he will have some rapid sucks to get the milk flowing, and then he will settle down into a steady, regular sucking rhythm.

> Sometimes mothers are not aware that there is a problem with their attachment.

His little nose will look squashed against your breast, but this is the way it is supposed to be. When his nose is squashed, he can breathe in more air.

Failure to latch on baby correctly can lead to sore nipples, a hungry baby, and poor weight gain. If baby is really struggling to latch on, it is helpful to go and see a Lactation Consultant. Even weeks or months down the track she will be able to identify any problems and help you to correct them. You can also check your attachment if your baby is not gaining weight. Sometimes mothers are not aware that there is a problem with their attachment.

### The First Few Days.

If he is sleepy during those first few days and weeks, stroking his cheek may help him keep going. Always strive to keep him awake while feeding, rather than let him doze off. If he falls asleep and you try to pull him off, he can hang on tight and do some damage to your nipples. If he stays and sleeps, it will prolong the feeding time while he snoozes and snacks. And that can be exhausting for mum over a period of time.

During those first few days, feeding will often take around 40 minutes – about 20 minutes a side. You can even alternate sides more frequently: 10-10-5-5 or similar to keep baby awake. Your baby will be tired after a feed, and probably just sleep until hungry again a couple of hours later. After a few days many babies wake up a little, and can start to feed more efficiently. Plan on a total of 30 minutes feedtime if possible, after those first few weeks. This will allow some time for baby to be awake after his feed, and you can enjoy time with him for a few minutes before putting him back to bed.

Another thing about that first day or two is that sometimes a baby will be especially sleepy, and unable to

> **I always recommend feeding on both sides at every feeding. This allows both breasts to be stimulated at every feed.**

be woken for a feed for a seemingly long time. Even up to 6-8 hours. If your baby does this in the first day, then it is usually OK. Perhaps he needs that sleep to recover from his delivery. After a day of sleep, he will probably be quite happy to be more awake and feeding.

If he becomes extra sleepy after two or three days, then that is different, and it's worth checking him out for jaundice, which can cause sleepiness.

*Two Sides of the Story...*

I always recommend feeding on both sides at every feeding. This allows both breasts to be stimulated at every feed. This may mean pulling baby off after 20 minutes on the first side (during those first few days), to allow him to have a turn on the other side. Otherwise he could spend 40+ minutes on one side, and not wake again for another 2 hours.

After that first week or two, baby should feed much more quickly. You will learn to judge when to pull him off in order to allow him to have some more on the other side. Some babies detach on their own to be burped and swapped, but others are hangers-on!

When you alternate each side that you start a feed on, you'll allow your breasts to feel fairly even in size. If you always start on the same side (which can happen for short periods if you have especially sore nipples or mastitis), then you may feel a little 'lopsided'.

*Letdown – Too Fast or Too Slow?*

When baby first begins to suck strongly at a feed, he is receiving the *foremilk*. This milk is sweet to encourage baby to suck strongly, but is not especially rich. Hopefully after just a few seconds, this foremilk is replaced by the richer *hindmilk*. This process is called the *letdown*.

> **Sometimes a mother will have an especially strong letdown reflex.**

Sometimes a mother will have an especially strong letdown reflex. This can mean that baby is squirted quite forcibly in the face soon after he starts to feed, and so he has enormous trouble swallowing. He can end up gulping air instead of milk.

Rather than keep baby on, sputtering and gulping air (which can lead to a tummy ache), it is helpful to pull baby off, once the letdown has occurred. Allow the milk to fall onto a cloth nappy or towel until the force of the flow subsides. Then put baby back on again, and allow him to finish his feed at a pace he can keep up with. Feeding while lying down is also sometimes recommended for a short time to help with this problem.

Sometimes a mother has a very slow letdown, and it can be frustrating for that hungry baby who wants that good milk right now!

It is important for mum to relax and take deep breaths while she is waiting for a slow letdown. Worrying and fussing with the baby is only going to prolong the time. Thinking about baby with closed eyes, deep breathing, and praying are all things that can help get that letdown reflex to kick in.

*Length of Feeds – Efficient Feeder or Lazy Sucker*

Some babies, like my baby Oliver, are super fast feeders – a baby can drain a breast in 5-7 minutes if he is efficient. Trying to make him feed longer often results in loud protests and back arching. If you are concerned about him not having had much milk, you can try giving him longer burp time, followed by another try on the other side after 10-20 minutes. As long as baby is happy after a feed and gaining weight, then fast feeding is usually fine.

Other babies, like my Madeline, are 'lazy suckers'. If your baby feeds for a long time on the first side, and then won't feed on the second side, then try timing him and pulling him off halfway. If he normally feeds 20 minutes on that first side, simply detach him (*gently*) after 10 minutes, give him a burp, and pop him on the other side to finish.

Try not to let these 'lazy suckers' feed all day – they are usually not feeding continuously, but 'sipping, snoozing and snacking'!

*Burping*

After a feed, your baby should look full and content. His eyes will often roll back in his head, and he might look a little 'drunk'! Time for burping...

There are several different ways to burp, and you will find the best position for your baby. Over your shoulder. Sitting on your knee with his chin supported by your hand. Lying across your lap on his tummy. Hard patting on the back. Gentle back rubbing.

Try not to spend a long time burping. If nothing has happened in 5 or 10 minutes, pop him on the floor to have a kick for a short time, and then try burping again a little later. Some babies are great little burpers, and others are more reluctant.

> **Try not to let these 'lazy suckers' feed all day – they are usually not feeding continuously, but 'sipping, snoozing and snacking'!**

## Feeding Routines

*How Long Between Feeds?*
It is important to always feed a hungry baby.

> **I have always chosen to feed my babies on a flexible routine, rather than just whenever they cried.**

It is not always easy however, to determine when a baby is actually hungry or when he is instead tired, unwell, or just needing a cuddle.

I have always chosen to feed my babies on a flexible routine, rather than whenever they cried, or at irregular intervals. In this way I have been certain that they are being fed, even if they have been sleepy. This has allowed my babies to be relaxed and content, knowing that their mother will feed them and they don't need to fuss for food. I have mostly (although not always) needed to wake my new babies in order to feed them.

This will mean feeding at around the 3 hourly mark in those first few days (meaning that it is around 3 hours from the time you start a feed, until the time you start another feed). I have chosen to wake my babies to feed them at this time during the day, rather than let them sleep for long periods. Tiring as it can feel at first, it has been much easier to feed them on this routine, than having the unpredictability of waiting until they wake up. And then wondering if they need a feed.

If your baby wakes a little earlier and is hungry, then he would need to be fed, of course.

However those first few days are an ideal time to try to feed him as close to that 3 hourly mark as possible. Once he gets into that pattern, he will probably quickly get used to it. Many mums find that their babies will then start to wake for a feed at around the same time.

If your newborn looks to be having good feeds, but is not sleeping well after a feed, then check that he is latching on correctly. He may also have bit of a tummy ache, rather than crying to be fed.

I have found all my babies have an unsettled day around day three or four, where they just haven't slept much all day. During this time I still try to feed them at fairly regular intervals, and spend much more time cuddling and soothing them than I might otherwise need to. After this bad day, they have always settled down again.

It isn't uncommon for a baby to have unsettled days now and again in those first few weeks. I suggest just keeping on doing what you need to do, and he will usually settle down again in a day or so. He may be a little hungrier than usual because your milk supply hasn't kept up with his growth spurt. Or perhaps he has been over-stimulated after a big day out, or had lots of extra cuddles with Grandma. Consistency, routine and maybe an extra feed or two will probably settle him down after a day or so.

> **It isn't uncommon for a baby to have unsettled days now and again in those first few weeks.**

If it does not, and your baby remains constantly unsettled, then it is time to seek some medical advice to rule out anything else that may be causing his discomfort.

I suggest mums consider trying to move their babies onto a 3½ hour routine around the 8-10 week mark if possible, and try to have them on a (approximately) 4 hourly routine around the 12-14 week mark. Some babies will take longer to stretch these times out, which is fine, and some babies will do it more quickly.

If your baby is still feeding 3 hourly at around 16-20 weeks, then he may begin to struggle with his sleep patterns, as he will require longer awaketimes.

*When is it Too Long – or Too Short Between Feeds?*

Some babies will go around the clock 3 hours or so for weeks (and months), and others will start to stretch at night from day one. It may be helpful to keep waking your baby through the night if he is very sleepy, and you are worried about your milk supply. Many babies soon start to stretch to 4-5 or so hours overnight. This is fine. Much longer than that in the very early weeks may mean mum needs to keep a closer eye on her supply.

If you are consistently feeding less than 2-3 hourly, it is helpful to consider why. Is baby hungry? Do you have to work on building up your milk? Is baby struggling to get into good sleep patterns? Do you have to work on sleep settling?

> **Some days call for more flexibility!**

Too close together (less than 2 hourly), is very exhausting for mum and often doesn't produce better results in milk supply than 3 hourly. In fact, many mums feeding every hour or two are just too tired to maintain a good milk supply.

*How Flexible is Flexible?*

Some mums find that while they have a regular 3 or 4 hourly routine during most of the day, they may need to add an extra feed or two closer together at the end of the day because their milk supply drops a little (sometimes referred to as 'cluster feeding'). This is fine. Make sure, though, that most of the feeds through the day are consistent in times.

Avoid a routine that goes 3 hours, 4 hours, 2 hours, 3½ hours etc. This is probably a little too flexible. A routine that goes (approximately) 3 hours, 3 hours, 3 hours, 2½ hours, 2½ (or similar) is OK, because for the most part of the day, the feeds are at fairly regular intervals.

Some days call for more flexibility!

Travelling, visitors, trips to doctors, Grandma's, church and shops all mean one of those flexible days. Relax and go with the flow from time to time. Perhaps baby will cope fine. Perhaps baby will be fussy the following day. Try to get back on track when you can.

Some babies cope quite well with a fairly flexible routine most days. They still eat and sleep well and are happy that their routine is a little loose. Other babies just don't cope so well unless their days are kept fairly tight. Sometimes babies who usually cope with a flexible day, become unsettled (due to extra busy days, illness etc.) and really benefit from a few days of tight routine until things get back on track.

As you get to know your baby, you will discover what works best in your family.

### Night Feeds

Night-time feeds require very little stimulation. Just a feed, burp, nappy change (if needed) and bed. Try keeping lights low, noise down, and otherwise as quiet as possible. This helps baby learn that night is for sleeping, not play!

> **How might you be confident that your milk supply is keeping up with your baby's needs?**

A late night feed (at around 10.30pm or so) can be helpful to cut down on night feeds. That way mum can stay up until that last feed, then go to bed knowing she may only need to get up once for the 2am feed before it is morning. However, if mum needs to go to bed early, and doesn't mind night feeds, then that's fine too!

## Breastfeeding for the Long Haul

### When the Supply Runs Low

Sometimes a mum goes through periods of lower milk supply. How might you be confident that your milk supply is keeping up with your baby's needs?

It is useful for a mum to keep a record of things like: the number of wet and dirty nappies, the number and length of feeds, and the weight and height gain of their baby. Visiting the local Early Childhood Clinic every couple of weeks for those first few months is helpful to allow baby to be accurately weighed. If baby is not putting on weight, or growing in height, then that might indicate that your milk supply is not keeping up. If baby suddenly starts waking hungry early for his regular feeds, or in the night (when he was previously sleeping longer), then that may also be an indicator. If baby does not seem satisfied after a feed – perhaps he is fussing – then he may still be hungry. Your baby should start 'filling out' around his body after a few weeks – creases in the arms and legs, and perhaps a double chin. If your baby is looking overly scrawny, then he may not be getting enough to eat.

If you suspect your milk supply is not doing so well, then there are a few things you can try to build it up again.

First, check that you are eating well and drinking lots of water. Check also that you are not rushing around doing too much, and that you are having a rest in the afternoon. Mums of several children are prone to over-doing things! Over-exercising is also a problem for some mums, and will jeopardise their supply from time to time.

Pumping after feeds is an effective way to increase your supply. Just pump for a few minutes after a feed, store in the fridge, and offer it to him after the next breastfeed. If you can do this up to three times a day, for around three to five days, you should notice a difference.

Other temporary methods of boosting supply include giving a top up feed before bed in the afternoon ('afternoon tea'), or adding another late evening feed, if you aren't already doing one.

Sometimes mums find vitamin (or even recommended herbal) supplements helpful to give a flagging milk supply a boost. Sustagen has worked wonders for me!

If your baby is having solids, *always* give milk first. Otherwise your baby may not be hungry enough to drink enough milk to keep up your supply.

*Can You Breastfeed for Longer than Six Months?*
Of course!

Mums choose to stop feeding for a variety of reasons. If you have a good milk supply, and you and your baby are happy to continue feeding, then there is no need to stop. Breastmilk continues to give your baby adequate nutrition until around 12 months.

> **If your baby is having solids, always give milk first.**

You can certainly continue to feed your baby beyond 12 months, but he will also eat more regular food and drink more fluids in addition to breastfeeds. While many babies will want solids from around 6 months or so, this is no reason to stop breastfeeding.

Some mums stop feeding because they have chosen to work either part or full time, because of pressure from family or friends, illness or pregnancy. These may all be valid reasons. However, the myth that breastfeeding is not possible, or too difficult beyond 6 months, is not true!

Some mums continue to pump milk for bottle feeds once going back to work full or part time. It takes dedication, but is very possible!

*What About Fertility?*
Many women have no menstrual cycles while they are breastfeeding their babies (or perhaps the first 9-12 months of feeding), meaning they are unlikely to fall pregnant. Other women however, discover their fertility returns quite soon after baby is born, so there are no guarantees!

Having babies very close together, while tiring for mum for a year or two, is not a disaster. The children are guaranteed to be great playmates as they grow up together!

*When to Wean?*

Sometimes mums need to wean their babies.

This might be because they need to go to work, or want to fall pregnant. Maybe because of illness, family upheaval, or for some other reason. If your baby has been a great feeder up to now, then this can be a little traumatic – for mum, as well as baby!

Many mums from 9 months onwards, find it easier to go straight to a sippy cup, rather than a bottle. At 9 months, most babies are able to manage a sippy cup quite well. Formula is recommended until around 12 months.

It is usually best to drop the feeds one at a time every few days, to prevent engorgement and mastitis. The midday feed is often the easiest to drop first, followed by the late afternoon feed. The last feed to go can be either the last night feed or the first feed. Some mums keep one or two breastfeeds for quite some time, and this can often work quite well. This could mean breastfeeding in the morning and/or evening, while giving formula (or cow's milk if baby is over 12 months) throughout the day.

Of course, there is no requirement to wean your baby at 9 or 12 or 18 months!

Feeding past 12 months is recommended by the World Health Organization, so keep going as long as is it convenient for you and your baby.

*Can you Breastfeed While Pregnant?*

A common 'wisdom' is that it is not possible to fall pregnant while you are breastfeeding. Many a mother will disprove this theory, though!

While it isn't very common, it is certainly possible for some mums to fall pregnant while still breastfeeding. I have! What to do?

Some mums are able and happy to continue feeding their baby throughout a pregnancy and beyond. This is no problem if mum is happy.

Some mums however, are very tired with their pregnancies. They may find that trying to maintain a milk supply, as well as a growing baby, as well as their own health and energy - becomes almost impossible.

Other mums (like me) become quite sick during a pregnancy, and can't manage feeding a baby, while feeling nauseous or even vomiting.

If you need to wean baby earlier than you had originally planned because of an unexpected pregnancy, then your baby will manage. And you might well feel so much better and able to cope with a pregnancy as well as a baby.

> **Some mums are able and happy to continue feeding their baby throughout a pregnancy, and beyond.**

### Bottlefeeding

There will be some mums who are bottle-feeding, either because they have chosen to do so, or because they found breastfeeding too difficult (for a variety of reasons).

Which formula is best? For most babies, it isn't going to matter a great deal – these days, they are all age-appropriate, nutritionally balanced and suitable for most babies. The exceptions will come if you or your baby is prone to severe allergies, when you may opt for soy, goat or another special milk. Check also that you have the correct teat for your baby (and that it has the correct size hole in the top).

> **Be careful not to put baby to bed with a bottle.**

Bottle-fed babies often gain weight a little faster than breastfed babies, and their nappies are smellier. In our western countries however, they can often be as healthy as those who are breastfed.

Consider moving to a cup after his first birthday, so that he doesn't become so attached to his bottle that he is unwilling to part with it. And be careful not to put baby to bed with a bottle. Research shows an increase in tooth decay in babies who have a bottle frequently in their beds. Likewise, avoid putting sugary juice in his bottle or allowing him to roam around the house with a bottle in his mouth.

## Extra bits

### Jaundice in Babies

It is not very uncommon for some babies to develop jaundice in the first few days after being born. Symptoms include sleepiness, reluctance to feed, and yellow skin. Some babies are more prone to this than others, and sometimes it arises for no apparent reason.

Sunlight and frequent feeds are recommended for a baby with jaundice. This might mean, after that first couple of days, that your sleepy baby will need to be woken quite frequently (every 2 hours) to be fed. This will help flush out the toxins. Some babies are put under lights in the hospital to help also. This can be quite distressing for mum, but is usually only short lived.

Most babies are fine after a few days of extra feeds and/or lights, so if this happens to you, hang in there and it should soon pass.

### Biting Babies!

A common problem can arise when baby decides to bite during feeding. Ouch!

Sometimes he might bite because he is teething, and his gums are sore. Sometimes he might be falling asleep and sort of crunch down as he nods off. Sometimes it is because he enjoys the attention he receives from mum!

Whatever the reason it is certainly NOT fun for mum! What to do?

If he is at the end of a feed, then perhaps simply pull him off, change sides, or finish up as the simplest way to deal with this.

A stern "No!" while pulling baby off can also shock him into stopping. He will probably cry loudly at being spoken to sternly by mum, and go back to feeding properly.

If that hasn't helped, sometimes a gentle flick on the cheek can make him aware of what he is doing, and help him to forget about biting.

Some mums have been contemplating weaning when baby starts to bite, and this habit just hastens that process! Most babies, especially the younger ones, can be redirected, and the biting stage becomes fairly short lived. So hang in there!

*Spitting Up*

Some babies regularly 'spit up' after a feed. This can range from a fairly small amount, to a huge gush of milk. If your baby spits up a fairly small amount, then it is probably nothing to be concerned about.

If your baby regularly produces a large volume of milk, then it is worth checking out.

Some babies can return a large quantity of milk simply because they have eaten too much (like mine!). If your baby is growing well, gaining weight and is happy after feeds, then he is probably fine. Most of mine have been 'happy chuckers', with no other problems (apart from frequent changes of clothes and cloth nappies draped everywhere...).

Some babies however, return a large amount of milk, and then struggle to gain weight. If this is your baby, then go and talk to your doctor or clinic sister about the options available to help your baby retain his feeds better.

## *Thar she blows…!*

All babies get wind. Some babies get it more than others. Sometimes they seem as if they might blow away like a burst balloon if you let them go!

Most of the time, gentle back rubbing or patting after feeds, some time to kick on a flat surface (like the floor) or carrying baby on his tummy over your arm will help things settle down.

If you are breastfeeding, you may find that some foods you are eating affect your baby's wind problems. Experiment a little with your food to find out which things are less troublesome for baby.

If things are not improving, and his sleeps are becoming disrupted from his tummy pains, then an over-the-counter medicine like Infacol may help things along a little. Chat to your clinic nurse or doctor if you feel things are unmanageable.

## *Introducing Solids*

From around 6 months, your baby will be ready to start some solids.

How will you know it is time? You may find that he is still hungry after a feed, even though you have a good milk supply. You may find him waking early from his sleeps and being hungry, where he was previously happy to sleep longer. You may find him waking in the night and hungry, despite his day routine going well.

If you are breastfeeding, it might be wise to check your milk supply. It may need a boost, which may mean that solids are not necessary just yet.

If you (or your doctor or clinic sister) decide that now is a good time to start solids, then go ahead and give it a try.

Some folks recommend starting with rice cereal, other folks suggest pureed vegetables (eg pumpkin, carrot, or fruit like banana). Your clinic sister will be able to provide you with plenty of information on suitable first solids.

Your baby will probably only have a few mouthfuls the first few times, but will gradually increase the amount he is willing to eat.

You may find that he spits his first mouthful straight out again. This is probably not because he doesn't like the taste, but because his reflexes are still underdeveloped. If you give it a few tries, but he is still having trouble swallowing, then perhaps leave it for a week or two before trying again. He may be more ready by then.

Or he may not. Some babies are just not ready for a few more weeks or months. Some hold out until close to 12 months of age.

If your baby is happy and healthy and gaining weight on your breastmilk, then he is probably fine. Check with your doctor if you are at all concerned.

If your baby is much younger than 6 months, you may be better to work on your milk supply before opting for solids. You may not want baby filling up on solids, at the expense of your milk supply!

One last important thing to remember about introducing solids: **always breastfeed first before giving solids to maintain your milk supply**.

# Chapter Ten

# Crying and Settling
## What do I DO when my Baby Cries?

Before we have our first baby, the sound of a baby crying might be a little irritating. Or it might make us feel like we have to rescue it. Or we may not even notice it.

But the sound of our own baby crying has an unexpected impact on us mums. Our own baby is different. No mother likes to hear their baby cry – whether they are a newborn or 12 years old!

The reality is that our babies will cry. Some babies cry a lot. Some babies don't cry much at all. But all babies cry sometime. Sometimes for good reason – they are tired, or hungry, or dirty or hurting. Sometimes because something is seriously wrong. How do we tell the difference? And what do we do when they **do** cry?

In this chapter, we are going to look at some different aspects of crying and settling:

**How do I Know he is Crying because he is Hungry?**

**How Much Crying is Too Much?**

**Help! My Baby Cries Every Evening!**

**Cutting to the Chase: Settling Baby**

**Reflux, Colic and Tresillian**

## How do I Know he is Crying because he is Hungry?

*Stop, Think, Pray, Act.*

It is always helpful when our babies and young children cry, to first stop and think.

**Reacting before thinking can sometimes lead to discovering that you missed the obvious!**

What are they supposed to be doing now? Is it time for a feed? Is it time for bed? Are they hot? Cold? Dirty?

If you are unsure what the problem may be, pray for wisdom and guidance. Then act – feed baby, put baby to bed. Change, burp or comfort baby.

Reacting before thinking can sometimes lead to discovering that you missed the obvious!

*Food? Or Sleep?*

Is baby hungry or tired?

If baby has just had a long sleep, and it is several hours since the last feed, then he is most likely hungry. So feed him!

It is never wise to listen to a hungry baby cry!

If baby has just had a feed a short time ago, then it is possible baby is tired and ready for bed. Putting him to bed is the best action.

But there may be other reasons to consider: wind pain, over/under stimulation, dirty nappy, hot/cold or even stuck.

If baby truly seems hungry at a time when he is supposed to be sleeping, then feed him and consider checking your milk supply. Perhaps it has run down a little and needs a boost. Perhaps baby is having a growth spurt. Perhaps baby is unwell. Perhaps you are unwell.

Feed baby and think through the reasons for him to be hungrier than usual. Most often it is temporary, and can be managed with an earlier, or an extra feed.

If baby does have a tummy pain, then frequent feeds can often cause more irritation. Efficient burping and occasionally an over-the-counter medication, can help their little tummies settle better. Again, check with your doctor.

### The Writing's on the...Fridge

Helpful advice for those early days: keep a record of feed times and stick them on the fridge.

Sometimes our days get busy and we get so tired, that we lose track of where we are up to. If you remember to jot down the time each occasion you feed, it will help you make decisions when you have forgotten what you are doing. This way, when baby is crying and your head is muddled, you can check the fridge and see where you are up to with your feeds and sleeps.

### Midnight Corridors and Washing Machines

Many stories are told of mum or dad pacing the corridors in the middle of the night to get a crying baby back to sleep. Or placing their bassinets on the washing machine to lull them to sleep. Or patting, patting, patting for months to get them off. Or cuddling, rocking, singing to sleep. Or even driving around in cars to get them off to sleep.

Many people, out of desperation, find themselves doing something like this on occasion. Some people find themselves dependent on something like this daily.

But most babies can be taught to go to sleep simply by putting them to bed, and allowing them to fall asleep on their own. While it is so tempting to allow them to fall asleep in our arms every time in those early days and weeks, it does them no favours and is not fun a few months down the track. While the occasional sleeping baby in arms is priceless to experience, making it the norm is another story.

> **Start out where you want to go and the habit will stick.**

Many babies have a little cry before they go off to sleep. Allowing him to expend a little energy in this way is fine. If he hasn't settled after 10 minutes or so, a cuddle and burp can do the trick.

If this becomes the norm during the day, the nights need be no different – thus no need to spend the dark hours pacing the floors. From time to time they get sick, or there are other unusual disruptions in the family and those may be times when long nights are necessary.

But night after night? That can be avoided. Start out where you want to go and the habit will stick.

### Checking the Supply Line

If baby is simply not settling to sleep one day then perhaps a feed can do the trick. Sometimes even a few days of frequent feeds seem to be the only way to settle a crying baby. Especially if they are having a growth spurt.

If things don't improve after a few days, then consider checking your milk supply and working to build it up again. Tips for building up supply can be found in Chapter Nine.

## How Much Crying is Too Much?

### The Town Crier

Some babies barely raise a whimper. They thrive on a stable routine with all their needs met by their parents, and never feel the need to protest. My little Rosie was like this. Quiet. Patient. Content. She still is.

Others are the Town Criers! They feel the need to protest everything despite all their needs being faithfully met. My young Elliot was a Town Crier. He just loved the sound of his own voice. He still does!

Once other factors have been considered, examined and dismissed, it may be possible you have a little Town Crier in the making. If so then it is possible that he will be tricky to pacify. Patience, perseverance and consistency will help him settle into a more tolerable level of protest. The more inconsistent and flexible his days, the more he may likely protest. So finding a pattern that works to keep him settled is helpful.

Don't despair - most of these babies do settle down in time and learn to protest a little less.

If your quiet baby **suddenly** becomes a Town Crier, then perhaps he needs to be checked for illness. Or perhaps he has had a growth spurt (and hence an extra feed or two will help). Or perhaps he has just had a busy week. Lots of consistency and patience will hopefully calm down your little one so that he can continue to be a little less complaining.

> **Don't despair- most of these babies do settle down in time, and learn to protest a little less.**

### Checking With the Doc

Sometimes a prolonged period of crying, or sudden frantic crying, or distressing high pitched screaming needs to be checked out by your local doctor. Perhaps it is just to rule out anything medical, or perhaps to confirm your suspicions. Never feel bad about checking with your doctor – that is what they are there for. Reassurance is very good to hear!

You might consider checking with your doctor if baby's crying is unusual and inconsolable, if he also has a temperature, or has stopped eating. Sometimes mothers need to be persistent until an answer is found, although serious medical conditions are thankfully quite rare.

### Dummies, Thumbs and Super Suckers

Dummies are really a personal decision for the parents. Some parents start out deciding they don't want one. Some of those change their minds. Other parents start out planning to use one but then find their baby refuses.

If you find a dummy helpful for settling your baby to sleep, then that is fine. Perhaps try to think ahead about any boundaries you may wish to have with a dummy down the track – whether to wean baby off it in the first few months, or allow him to have it as long as he wishes. Whether to use it only for going to bed, or for awaketimes, car trips and such as well. Whether to get up and put it back in through the night, or train him to settle without it.

How might you wean your baby off his dummy?

Some folks go cold turkey, throwing out the dummy and managing an unhappy day or two until baby learns to settle himself.

Other folks do a slow wean – limiting the dummy to putting baby to bed initially, but not putting it back if it falls out. Or putting baby to bed without a dummy, but putting it back in to resettle if baby wakes up during a nap.

Some use the method of only ever buying newborn size dummies, so that baby finds it too difficult to keep sucking as he gets bigger, and gives up naturally. I found this one quite effective.

Likewise, thumbs (or fingers) can be adored by some babies. Often there isn't much mum can do if her baby finds his thumb, and it can be helpful for settling. The bigger problem comes when baby gets older and finds it a difficult habit to break. As we discovered with some of ours!

As far as weaning thumbs go, once baby is older (around 18 months – 2 years), you can start to teach him that his thumb is for bed, by gently pulling his thumb out of his mouth with a quiet "not now". And if thumb sucking is associated with a particular loved item – sheet, teddy, or even ribbon – then limiting that item to bed, and even eventually eliminating it altogether, will cut down on thumb sucking through the day.

Some babies are happy not to suck on anything at all, but there are babies that just love sucking on something – be it dummy, thumb, fingers or anything they can grab!

## Help! My Baby Cries Every Evening!

*Fussy Time and Arsenic Hour*

There is a pretty good chance that if your baby is fussing during the late afternoon/ evening, he isn't the only one! Babies are notorious for struggling to sleep well during this time of the day. A friend of mine used to call this "Arsenic Hour"!

> There is a pretty good chance that if your baby is fussing during the late afternoon / evening, he isn't the only one!

Sometimes this is because your milk supply has dropped through the day and baby is hungrier than usual. Sometimes it is because he has been over-stimulated through the day (especially if you have had a busy day in-and-out), and he is too wound up to sleep. And sometimes there doesn't seem to be a reason.

You can try resettling as normal and see if he eventually goes to sleep. You can try offering several closer feeds in this time, to see if he is truly hungry and it helps him settle. Or if all else fails, you can try popping him in his rocker chair for 15 minutes or so (they are often happy to sit quietly in a chair and watch the family activity for a short time), and then give him another go at trying to sleep.

Another if-all-else-fails management (especially if mum is tired and stressed, and it is late in the day) is to relax, pop him over your shoulder, and spend a couple of hours quietly sitting on the lounge. Perhaps watch TV or read a book, and allow him to catch up on some much needed sleep. As long as he doesn't become dependent on always needing this to get to sleep, then a few nights on your shoulder for an hour or two is fine for baby. And a chance for mum to smell him and enjoy him!

### When the Milk Goes Slow

When your milk is slowing down, and baby is inconsolable, stop and give him a feed. This is another good time to check your supply and see what you may be able to do to boost it again.

### Cluster Feeding

This is a common term for feeding closer together at the end of the day because supply is low. Some babies require a cluster feeding system for weeks or even months, especially if mum is busy and simply unable to keep her supply going through the day, despite her efforts.

It is helpful to try to keep the feeds as consistent as possible though, rather than all over the place. Regular 2½-3 hourly through the afternoon for a newborn for example, rather than just whenever baby cries. This allows mum to continue to do those important evening jobs of looking after her husband, family, dinner and all those other things that happen at this time, without the unpredictability of second guessing baby.

### Eat While the Meal is Hot

> **A helpful tip: give baby a nice warm bath just before his late night feed.**

If baby is regularly difficult to settle over the dinner period then consider prioritising your own family meal, rather then always skipping dinner to resettle, or tag teaming with hubby. Baby will be ok for 10 minutes or so while you have a hot meal together, and may even use that little extra time to resettle himself.

### Relaxing in a Hot Tub (the baby, that is!)

A helpful tip: give baby a nice warm bath just before his late night feed. This is a great job for dads, and it can help to relax baby, so that he has a lovely full feeding and settles into a long night sleep.

Then if you feel the need to have a nice long bath as well, go ahead!

## Cutting to the Chase: Settling Baby

*Unsettled Sleeps*

If you are sure your baby is well fed and therefore not hungry, then it is possible he is over-tired.

This is probably the most common reason that babies cry – they get over stimulated easily, and they struggle to get themselves to sleep. A tired baby will often go to sleep initially, but then wake into his sleep and cry, unable to go back to sleep.

Once a baby starts crying into his sleep, first check the clock – is it nearly feed time? If yes, then feed!

If it hasn't been long since the last feed, and you are sure he isn't hungry, then it may be time to start resettling.

Consistency is always the key.

I usually suggest going in every 10-15 minutes or so. This will depend on the age of the baby. Younger babies – up to 6-8 weeks or so – might need to be settled every 5-10 minutes. Pick up baby, soothe him, and put him back down for another 15 minute stretch. Sometimes you may need to spend quite a few minutes calming him down if he is really screamy – be patient.

Consistency with this usually works after a few days.

The first day is the hardest, until baby gradually works out that he is supposed to be sleeping. By the end of a week, most babies are sleeping much better, with maybe one or two protest sleep cycles/day.

> **Remember: we are training baby to put himself back to sleep on his own.**

Now and then they may fuss on and off through to the next feed, sometimes they may stay awake but happy, and mostly they learn to go back to sleep.

Remember: we are training baby to put himself back to sleep on his own.

This skill will help for night-time waking also. If baby has been waking at night, then he will nearly always have a day waking problem that needs to be addressed first (whether it be feeding related, or routine/resettling problems). Once he can settle himself during the day, the night usually sorts itself out.

If you suspect he is in pain/not feeling well etc, then get him checked out for your peace of mind.

All parents are going to need to resettle their babies at some point. No baby is perfectly settled all the time. As a mum it is a good idea to decide on a plan and stick to it as much as possible, rather than change tactics every day. This will only confuse your baby.

### Unsettled Awaketimes

The most common reason for a baby to be grumpy during his awaketime, is over-tiredness. He has been fed, had a play and been happy. But now he is now fussing - he is probably ready for bed.

The solution? Wrap him up (if he is still little), and put him to bed!

What if he is really grumpy? Perhaps you are out, or at Grandma's, or had a busy day, and he is really, really cranky. Then be sure to soothe him and calm him in your arms, before you lay him down to sleep. He will need to feel calm and secure as he goes down, or he will struggle to relax enough to go to sleep.

I do feel sorry for tiny babies when I see their parents bouncing them on their knees trying to cheer them up, when they are so obviously tired!

Another reason for grumpy awaketimes can be a baby that has learned to be constantly "entertained".

This is often a baby that has enjoyed the attention of the family and protests loudly when he is ignored, even for a short time. Often these babies are charming when they are getting attention, but very noisy when they are left alone. When they cry and someone fusses over them, it continually reinforces the pattern that has been created.

If this sounds familiar, don't despair! You can teach your baby to become more content without the need for constant attention.

**You can teach your baby to become content without the need for constant attention.**

Gradually extend your time away from baby, so that he learns to not be dependent on those around him for his entertainment. Start with a minute or two, and extend that over time and as he gets bigger. Try not to continually gush over him when he has cried for your attention, but be calm and positive when coming back into his visual circle.

Some babies are just so social that they will always love constant attention. Give him lots of attention, but remember to balance it with teaching him that he can enjoy his own company for little stretches too.

The pattern of **play alone, play near mum,** and **play with mum** is also helpful for this baby. It creates a balance in his day so that he gets plenty of attention, but it is balanced between playing alone and playing near others.

# Reflux, Colic and Tresillian

## *Reflux – Behavioural or Medical?*

Reflux is a form of heartburn in babies that can cause pain during and after feeding, and therefore crying.

It is usually identified by excessive crying during and after feeding and diagnosed by a doctor or clinic sister on the basis of information given by mum. Gastro oesophageal reflux is caused by an immature valve in the oesophagus allowing acid from the stomach to come back up. Reflux is more common in bottle-fed babies, and is usually out-grown by 6-12 months of age.

A baby diagnosed with reflux will often benefit from having his bed raised slightly at the head to stop acid building up in his oesophagus. These babies don't usually like to lie flat on their backs for too long after a feed, and will rather enjoy sitting up in a rocker chair instead. They can struggle with feeding as it is uncomfortable for them to lie down and feed, so mum needs to be patient with her baby. Some mums find that feeding baby while standing up (possibly using a sling for added support) is helpful.

Spitting up after feeds does not necessarily mean that reflux is a problem – many healthy babies spit up after feeds. Excessive or projectile vomiting however, may be a sign of reflux worth investigating, especially if accompanied by frequent crying and slow weight gain.

A baby with reflux also needn't alter his routine of feed/wake/ sleep. There is no need to allow him shorter sleeps or  longer awaketimes. This will only lead to a tired and grumpy baby, who will become even more frustrated at feedtime. If he is struggling with his naps, try patiently and calmly resetting him and being as consistent as possible with his routine.

If your baby is on a consistent routine with appropriate awaketime lengths, and is still regularly crying during and after feeds, then it is worth investigating further to find a cause.

Yes it can be a real disease, and if your doctor suspects reflux, he (as well as your local pharmacist) should recommend some medication that causes a fairly miraculous change in baby's crying patterns.

If medication has made little difference, or if your doctor is unwilling to suggest any medication, then it may be possible that your baby's crying has causes other than reflux.

### Colic – a Disease or a Symptom?

Colic is a well-known explanation for excessive or continual crying in young babies. However it is usually more of a description of inconsolable crying than a medical condition itself. Sometimes colic can be blamed for what is actually wind pain, reflux, over-stimulation or tiredness. It is especially common during the 2-4 month period.

Once a good routine, resettling techniques and healthy milk supply are implemented, many cases of colic settle down. If you are concerned about your baby's inconsolable crying, then of course see a doctor to discuss whether there is a medical reason for his distress.

### Tresillian – Necessary?

Sometimes mothers are referred to Tresillian (or a similar live-in facility for new mothers and babies) for help with their babies. Most often Tresillian will help a mother put her baby onto a predictable, though flexible routine, and give her the confidence to manage her own baby. It can also help mum get back on track if she is struggling with Post Natal Depression.

Sometimes mum and baby have lost their routine, and constant crying and sleeplessness can make decision-making difficult. Sometimes mothers are so confused by all the 'helpful' voices, that they are simply unable to make decisions without some outside help.

If you are struggling, need help, and are unable to find helpful support, then it is an option available to you. They may be helpful in walking you through the days of baby feeding and sleeping, while allowing you to catch up on some much needed sleep.

Tresillian also has phone help lines. If you are struggling to make sense out of conflicting advice, then this is another option available. The downside to seeking advice from a helpline is that it is yet another opinion! If a mum tries every piece of advice she hears, she will undoubtedly be very confused. And so will baby. Sometimes it is better to stay on a course of action, and minimise the voices.

> **If a mum tries to follow every piece of advice she hears, she will undoubtedly be very confused!**

# Chapter Eleven

# Sleeping
## When the Sleep Ain't so Sweet!

There is nothing quite so calming as a sleeping baby. When we see little babies asleep in their prams, we mums can go weak at the knees! It would be nice to think that they are always like that, but reality is often different! Some babies don't like to sleep much at all, and all babies will have their moments of sleeplessness.

In this chapter, we will look at the following areas:

**How Long does a Baby Sleep Anyway?**

**How do I Put Him to Sleep?**

**How do I Keep Him Asleep?**

**Night Owls and Snoozers**

**Managing Illness**

## How Long does a Baby Sleep Anyway?

*Understanding Sleep Cycles*

Babies (and people in general), tend to follow a cyclical pattern of sleep. They move through different phases – light (REM) sleep, and then deep sleep. During their light (or active, or dreaming) sleep phase, they will often flutter

> **Babies, and people in general, tend to follow a cyclical pattern of sleep.**

their eyes and even move their arms, legs and head. They are fairly easy to wake up when they are in this stage, and some babies can be too easily woken! When they are in a deep sleep phase, they are very still, and hardly appear to be breathing. These cycles follow a pattern of around 40-50 minutes each.

One of the aims of the first few weeks and months is to help your baby move through these cycles as calmly as possible. Sometimes babies get stuck and wake during the light sleep cycle. If they are not hungry, they may well need some help to resettle back into the sleep pattern that has been disrupted. If these cycles are always disrupted, they may have real difficulty resettling themselves during night sleeps, and so wake at fairly regular intervals (of 45-60 minutes).

Understanding your baby's sleep patterns will be helpful to determine the cause of waking during sleeps and find the best way to manage his waking.

### The Sleepy Baby

Some babies like my Rosie, are very sleepy for the first few weeks and even months. This could be because of a traumatic birth, prematurity or personality. It may also be due to illness or jaundice, so it is worth keeping an eye on, and mentioning to a clinic sister if your baby is still struggling to wake for feeds after the first month or so.

Sometimes a 3 hourly routine is just too difficult for a sleepy baby to manage, and a longer routine of up to around 4 hours or so works better. Allowing him a slightly longer stretch between feeds can mean that he is more alert for those feeds and thus feed better, rather than have mum continually trying to keep him awake.

> **Over-tired babies will very often struggle to sleep well.**

These sleepy babies often need shorter awaketimes, but may have one awaketime in the day when they are awake for much longer (to catch up!).

It is not uncommon for a sleepy new baby to sleep up to eighteen - twenty hours a day.

*When the Party Goes On (... and on...)*

Other babies are party animals! They seem to thrive on no sleep and want to be part of the action 24/7.

These babies take a little more work to get into good sleep patterns. Perseverance is necessary, and perhaps a little understanding that they may have slightly longer awaketimes than those sleepy babies. Not too long though, or he will quickly unravel, and you may be back to night waking again! Rather than waiting for 'tired signs' before every sleep, understand that sometimes these babies just don't show signs of tiredness until it is well and truly too late. And by then those tired signs are over-tired signs. And over-tired babies will very often struggle to sleep well.

Try to anticipate his need for bed before he gets too wound up, despite his nature to keep on enjoying the action. Newborns should rarely be up for more than an hour.

Even a more alert newborn should try to get sixteen - eighteen hours sleep each day until they get a little bigger.

*Can you Wake a Sleeping Baby?*

If you are going to keep your baby on a flexible routine, then it will be necessary to wake a sleeping baby sometime. If baby isn't woken for regular feeds during the day, then it will take longer to get him into a predictable routine. He typically can fall into a pattern of having his days and nights mixed up, which can lead to him having trouble sleeping through the night.

Sometimes you will let baby sleep. If you have had a big day, and baby hasn't had much sleep, you may let him sleep a little longer. If baby is unwell and frequently unsettled, you may let him go a little longer. If you are trying to

> **Some babies will always need to be woken because they love their sleep, and others will never need to be woken because they love their food!**

stretch the feeds from say, 3 hours to 3½ hours, you will let your baby sleep longer.

Some babies will always need to be woken, because they love their sleep, and others will never need to be woken, because they love their food!

### *When Grandma Comes to Visit*

This is a time for flexibility with your routine. Unless, of course, Grandma lives with you or spends every day at your house 'helping with the baby'!

If Grandma is an occasional visitor to your home, then she will be very disappointed if baby is always whisked off to bed with never a cuddle. It will not hurt baby to have a day of cuddles with Grandma, and will make Grandma's day.

If Grandma (or other important family member or friend) is a frequent visitor to your home, then perhaps some boundaries may need to be considered so that Grandma understands that baby needs to have some time in his own bed.

Relationships are important, so consider Grandma's feelings. One day you will be the Grandma!

## How do I Put Him to Sleep?

### *To Rock or Not to Rock?*

Rocking a baby to sleep is an unforgettable experience! There is nothing as emotionally powerful as rocking your own baby to sleep.

> **As a training tool to teach baby to get to sleep, regular rocking has a few problems.**

And in the first few weeks, it can be so very tempting. After all there isn't much else to do with him! However as a training tool to teach baby how to always get to sleep, it has a few problems.

Six months into rocking baby to sleep before **every** sleep (and nap and bedtime and through the night), mum is exhausted and the fun has worn off. It is far better to teach baby to go to sleep on his own than be bound to rocking baby in order for him to fall asleep.

Occasional rocking to sleep is fine – like when you are out or baby has been particularly unsettled or you have visitors- but aim for saving it for a special occasion rather than **every** occasion.

There is a way to teach him to go to sleep on his own: put baby to bed **awake** rather than allow him to always fall asleep in your arms, or while feeding.

If he becomes dependent on falling asleep in mum's arms, then it will become very demanding on mum to be there all the time. Some mums don't mind, but most mums eventually decide that it would be easier on the whole family if they didn't have to spend so much time in their day (and night) getting their babies to sleep.

Again, rocking is is fine from time to time. Just not every time.

### The Caterpillar Wrap

Picture a caterpillar wrapped tightly in a cocoon with just his little head poking out. This is how very young babies love to be wrapped - nice and tight. Wrapping sends a message to a newborn that it is time for sleep, and they love the comfort of being so snug. Unwrapped newborns startle easily, and wrapping him stops this from happening so often when he is just falling asleep. Always wrap his arms up around his head but inside the wrap, or he will struggle to free them.

> **Wrapping sends a message to a newborn that it is time for sleep.**

If it is hot weather, then use a single layer of muslin or cheesecloth, over a singlet and nappy, to keep him a little cooler.

I had a couple of summer babies who needed a much thinner wrap than my winter babies.

Once they get to around 4 months old many babies are just about done with wrapping, and now prefer to be free. Perhaps a loose wrap is plenty- just to signify sleeptime. Other babies prefer to be wrapped for a little longer, and some even go for 12 months in a wrap. Rosie liked being wrapped until she was 6 months. Elliot clung to his wrap until he was over 2!

SIDS guidelines discourage mothers from putting babies to sleep on their tummies, and encourage putting them to bed on their back. If baby sleeps on his back every sleep, he may develop a flat head. This is not dangerous, and he will regain his round head shape eventually. If baby is going to sleep on his side, then alternating sides each sleep will stop that lop-sided flat head look.

### Own Bed or Mummy's Bed?

Some families prefer a co-sleeping arrangement where baby sleeps with mum. Some mums find it easier to feed during the night when they don't actually have to get out of bed.

There are a few problems with co-sleeping, though.

Co-sleeping encroaches on dad's space. It will reduce opportunities for intimacy between mum and dad. It can mean less sleep for mum – as she becomes aware of every snuffle baby makes. And there can be great difficulty in transitioning baby into his own bed at some point down the track.

Some families keep baby in mum's room so that access is easier during the night. This can work fine for some families but again, babies can be quite noisy as they sleep and some mums find they are constantly being woken up by baby noises. New mums are amazingly tuned in to every sound their baby makes! If your house is tiny and rooming-in is necessary, then that is something to manage as best as possible. We tried it for a while with Sebastian, but it didn't give me peace and quiet in the night – he was rather noisy!

Other families keep baby in a separate bedroom from mum and dad, especially during the night. This allows mum to hear important noises – like a hungry baby's cry – while sleeping through the baby snuffles. And it means that mum can get up to feed baby in the night without waking up a dad who needs to go to work the next day.

In the end it is a personal choice. It was not our preference to sleep with our babies in our bed each night. But of course every family is free to make these decisions for themselves.

Sleeping in a separate bed or room will not disadvantage your baby, and it can allow mum and dad some space of their own. If you are juggling other children and bedroom space, you can try keeping baby in your room for day sleeps, and in the lounge room (or somewhere else) at night. At least until they sleep through the night, and are less likely to wake up sleeping siblings. We did this with all of our babies and it worked very well for us all.

### A Drink Before Bed?

Feeding baby to sleep can be quite comforting for mum and baby, but isn't particularly helpful for long term settling. If you want your baby to learn to self-settle, then feeding him to sleep on a regular basis will delay this skill.

> **If you want your baby to learn to self-settle, then feeding him to sleep on a regular basis will delay this skill.**

Some occasional exceptions may include: the very sleepy newborn, the premmie, the unwell baby, the very over-tired baby, or a time of needing to boost supply with a sleepy, late-night feed.

### When they Protesteth Too Much!

Some babies just don't want to go to bed. Ever.

They protest even when you are only **thinking** about putting them to bed! These babies take a little patience and plenty of consistency with their bedtime routines. Doing the same things every time at bedtime is helpful. Remember: tight wrap (for those little babies), a cuddle, and then down to sleep.

Allow him to protest for a set amount of time – maybe 5-10 minutes or so, then give him a cuddle and back rub until he calms down, and then pop him back to bed. Limit stimulation – talking, jiggling, bright lights, constant unwrapping, unnecessary nappy changes, playing. My Elliot was a bedtime protester. And he did get better over time!

These babies (providing there is no underlying cause for their crying, like hunger or illness) do settle down eventually, so patience!

## How do I Keep Him Asleep?

### When they Wake Early

When baby wakes before feedtime, it is always helpful to stop and think before reacting.

**Consistency is the key.**

Is it feed time? Or nearly feed time? Does he usually wake early?

Is it a hot/cold day? Did he have a long awaketime and may be over stimulated?

If you believe baby is hungry, then feed baby. If baby is waking early and hungry for every feed, then it may be time to check your milk supply.

If you suspect that baby is just unsettled, then it is worth trying some resettling techniques…

### Resettling Techniques

Consistency is the key. If you try something one day, and then something different the next day, or if you just keep changing the rules in the way you manage your crying baby, your baby will become confused and even more unsettled.

Try giving baby 5 or 10 minutes to see if he will settle himself off to sleep, before going in. If after that time, he is still protesting loudly, then go in to check on him. If he isn't stuck or dirty, then you can start resettling.

**It would not be unusual to need to resettle a young baby several times a day.**

Pick baby up, and gently rock or rub his back until he calms down. Often baby will stop crying immediately, and even smile – so delighted to be up!

Once he is calm, try putting him back down again. Baby is often not happy to be put back down, and may cry immediately. I suggest leaving him for another 10-15 minutes to see if he will settle again. A younger baby (under 3 mths) a little less time.

Leaving too little time between settling may not give him quite long enough to settle. But leaving him too long can be distressing for baby, mum, dad and the neighbours!

Allowing baby to just cry himself to sleep over a long period of time (greater than 15 or 20 minutes) is not helpful either. Go in regularly to check, calm and try again. This gives you the confidence to know that you are helping baby to settle, rather than abandoning him.

If baby's cries are inconsistent during that settling time – for example, he is starting and stopping his cry, or grizzling more than crying then it is wise to be more cautious about going in and possibly stirring him up, when he may have been close to dropping off to sleep.

Hopefully with some consistency baby will learn to fall asleep on his own, and these times of resettling become less common. It would not be unusual to need to resettle a young baby several times a day. Resettling all day every day however is unusual. If baby is really struggling, it may be time to look at other causes for his unsettledness.

### Going Out

It is going to be inevitable that you will take baby out during normal sleep times at some point.

This isn't much of a problem when they are very tiny and they sleep anywhere. As they get bigger however, they may not be content to stay asleep. Some outings are unavoidable (eg doctor's appointments), but some can be timed around baby's normal awaketime (like shopping trips). Give baby a feed before popping down to the shops, so that he can go back to bed when you get home.

If baby is able to fall asleep on his own, then taking a portable cot, sling or pram on extended outings will give him a familiar environment to fall asleep in. If baby is stubborn and refuses to sleep anywhere but his own bed in his own house, then some patience may be required. These babies may need to be kept home more often than taken out. And perhaps they just need to have shorter awaketimes for the remainder of the day after a big morning out to catch up.

Perhaps you could give him one of his day sleeps in a portable cot at home, just to give him some practice at sleeping somewhere other than his bed, so that he may be more adaptable when you take him out.

Some babies (usually numbers two and beyond) cope quite well when they are picked up out of their beds during a sleep, plopped in the car and driven to school/preschool, driven home and plopped back to bed. Many of these babies may have their day routines planned around the 9am and 3pm school trips every day. They can learn to be flexible- especially if we don't fuss over them!

*Flexibility*

Flexibility means recognising the context of a situation, and making temporary changes to adapt.

It doesn't mean being so flexible that baby has no consistency in his day. It does mean that when there are visitors, travel, holidays, unusual events, sickness in the house, ultra hot/cold days or anything other than the ordinary, you may make small changes in his normal feed and sleep patterns to fit in with the people around you, and with baby.

> **Some babies do well on a rather loose routine while others prefer a tighter routine to their day.**

Perhaps baby needs an extra feed or shorter sleeps to manage a situation. Perhaps longer sleeps. Perhaps none!

The key is to recognise it as temporary, and work at getting back on track once things get back to normal again.

Again, some babies do well on a rather loose routine while others prefer a tighter routine to their day.

*Tip Toe Through the Tulips…*

Some families, in an effort to do the best thing for their baby's sleep, insist on tiptoeing around the house during baby's naps. Or putting signs on doorbells. Or turning down the phone. Or insisting visitors whisper in the house.

Unfortunately what they are often doing is training their baby to sleep in total silence. Once that silence is broken, or there are situations where that silence cannot be controlled by mum and dad, baby will not sleep.

It is far better for baby, and for family and visitors, that baby learns to sleep with a small amount of background noise. If this is tricky to organise (like with a first baby), try putting on a radio (with a mix of talking and music) softly in the background (for a few days), and gradually raise the volume until baby is content to sleep through a moderate amount of noise. Then when noisy visitors drop in or the phone or doorbell rings, baby will not startle in his sleep and wake up.

Younger children in larger families learn early on to sleep through all the noise that a large family creates. It is definitely a learned skill!

## Night Owls and Snoozers

*When Night is Day*

Some babies decide that they would like to party at night and sleep through the day.

> Some babies decide that they would like to party at night and sleep through the day.

One way to avoid this happening is to wake baby regularly during the day, rather than allow him to sleep too long.

When he is awake for night feeds, keep the lights low, the noise low, and stimulation low. Just a feed and change then back to bed with as little fuss as possible. Allow him to fuss for a few minutes when putting him down, rather than encouraging night partying by constant rocking, cuddling, pacing, patting, shushing and the like.

*The Snoozer – Stretching Day Sleeps*

Some babies sleep quite well through the night, but only snooze during the day.

This can continue on for days or even weeks, before the nights start to unravel. Good night sleep is often dependent on good day sleeps. So if your little one has decided a quick snooze is all he needs (and you are sure he isn't hungry), it may be time to train him otherwise.

Typically, they will wake around 45 minutes after they have fallen asleep. They may truly believe they have had enough sleep and need to get up and join the party. They are often bright-eyed and rearing to go. Many mothers discover however, that they fall apart after 20 minutes or so. Then mum wonders if they are hungry again, when they are probably actually tired.

> **Some babies sleep quite well through the night, but only snooze during the day.**

If you have already tested and ruled out hunger, he might benefit from a little sleep training...

Once he wakes up after 45 minutes or so, you can try to leave him to fuss for 5-10 minutes or so. Then go in, pick up baby (who by now is quite indignant at being kept in bed when he really wanted up), give him a quick soothe until he calms down (usually fairly quickly), and then put him back to bed to try again.

Often by this stage, they will protest immediately. However, after another 10-15 minutes or so, another soothe, and another go at resettling, many babies start to get the idea. A day or three of this type of resettling is often quite successful at teaching them to go back to sleep after their day snoozes. But as always, it will take commitment and patience from mum.

*Expectations versus Reality*

When we have our babies, we never expect things not to be perfect.

We don't count on how tired we will be, and how that will cloud our thinking and judgment, and how much our emotions will affect our decision-making.

We can feel overwhelmed with guilt if things aren't working out how we anticipated. If we can't breastfeed effortlessly. If our baby is unsettled.

Sometimes it is just helpful to know that every baby struggles with feeding and sleeping sometime, and that doesn't mean that you are a bad mother, or that baby necessarily has a serious problem. Many parts of baby's day will take some training, some practice and lots of patience. So hang in there!

> **Mothers have been raising babies since the beginning of time. You can do this!**

It is so very normal for any mum to feel fatigued while caring for a baby. It is hard work! So don't feel that you are failing because you are tired. Expect there to be bad days from time to time, and relax knowing that your baby will settle down in due course. Let some of your expectations go. Seek help and support from trusted friends, wise relatives or even professionals if it is needed. And share your struggles with others going through similar things.

This is of course how we learn best, and how we have always learned best. Mothers have been raising babies since the beginning of time. You can do this!

### When Hopelessness Sets In

Sometimes after a few bad days or weeks (even months), a sense of hopelessness can set in with mum and dad. Baby is crying too much and not sleeping enough. Mum is exhausted and feeling depressed. The whole household may be suffering.

Where to start?

Firstly, managing BABY...

A plan for your day, based on a flexible routine, will give you a foundation for managing your baby. If your day is chaotic, unpredictable and inconsistent, you will struggle to feel like you are getting on top of things. So getting baby settled is the first step.

Basically, baby needs a constant routine of **feeding**, then a time of being **awake**, then a time of **sleep**.

This happens for those new babies at around 3-4 hour intervals, depending on age. Under 3 months, will be around 3 hours or so, over 3 months working towards 4 hours. After 6-8 months you can start stretching out a little more to start fitting in with family mealtimes. Not: feed, sleep, feed, wake, feed, sleep, feed, whatever.... Baby needs to settle into a comfortable rhythm. And you will feel better once *you* are in a comfortable rhythm also.

> **Basically, baby needs a constant routine of feeding, then a time of being awake, then a time of sleep.**

Check that your milk supply is keeping up. Try some resettling techniques to help baby settle better on his own.

Looking after YOU is the next step...

Have a break out of the house from time to time if you haven't been getting out much.

Stay home a little more if you have been out every day.

Enlist the help of those around you if they have offered, but you have felt too proud to let them ("I can do it on my own!").

Go for a walk in the fresh air to clear your head. Have some chocolate, or a long hot bath. Snuggle up with hubby on the lounge.

And if that despair just doesn't shift and a big black cloud begins to descend on you, see your doctor. Post Natal Depression does happen, and to the best of mothers. There is no need to continue to suffer alone when help is available.

## Managing Illness

Most babies get sick from time to time – that is life. How do we manage our babies when they are unwell?

Over the course of six children we have experienced colds, flu, pneumonia, viruses, unexplained and mysterious infections requiring hospitalisation, asthma, eczema, tummy bugs, diarrhoea, vomiting, chicken pox, croup, head injury, ear and throat infections, kidney abnormalities, cuts, bruises, sprains and probably other various things that I have forgotten! It did take us thirteen years before we saw a broken bone! (Boy. Tree. Arm...!) This is just life with kids, and hopefully will never get more serious. Some families have more than their fair share of illness and injury, and will inevitably end up learning to manage as best they can.

### Managing Baby when He is Sick

Any time that you suspect illness, go and see your Doctor. High or persistent temperatures, excessive sleepiness, disinterest in feeding, unusual crying, vomiting, diarrhoea, and other unusual symptoms are all worth checking out.

When managing a baby through illness it is often necessary to feed him more frequently, to cuddle him more often, and to allow him to sleep longer. A day with a sick baby is very exhausting for mum – you can spend all day cuddling and feeding that baby (and not much else) and still feel wiped out at the end.

A teething baby can have also have a few days of feeling grumpy and miserable.

It is important to stay home when your baby is sick. This can be frustrating for mum, especially if it takes some time before baby is well again. Think of it as an opportunity to catch up on missed night sleep if you can snatch a snooze in the afternoon, or even a chance to finish that book you have been trying to read while baby is sleeping.

If you end up in the hospital it will be a difficult few days of travelling, sleeping in an uncomfortable chair and trying to represent 'normality' to your baby. Hang in there – hopefully this time will quickly pass and life can return to normal again.

*Managing Baby when He is Well Again*

For most parents, the next challenge can come with getting the baby back on routine after he has recovered from his illness.

It is easy to give some little concessions to our babies when they are sick – letting them sleep in our bed, or rocking them to sleep, or feeding them whenever they cry. And all these things may be ok for the short time they are sick. But there comes a day when you realise that he is no longer sick, but is still demanding all of that special attention.

Parents can choose to either gradually wean them off these extra snuggles or feeds, or go cold turkey and instantly try to do things the way you did before baby was ill. Either way, he may not be happy to go back to normal and it will take a few days. Allowing things to go on for months after he is well, only leads to tired and frustrated parents, and demanding babies and toddlers.

Sleeping is probably the most difficult thing to get back on track. Consistency and patience (and a little understanding) will triumph eventually, so stick with it!

## Dads Need Sleep Too!

Feeding in the night is very tiring for mum.

It can also be tiring for Dad, and if he is to get up and go to work the next day, he will eventually need to get some sleep.

For this reason, I usually suggest to mums that if dad is working, he shouldn't be required to be on night duty every single night. When baby wakes in the night, try not to expect dad to be up with you for all those feeds, every night. Let him rest so that he can be fresh and full of energy for his working day. He may then still have enough sparkle to be willing to help out in the evenings.

In our house dad would bath our little babies at around 11pm, then bring them in to me to feed and put to bed for the night. If baby woke during the night, I would normally go and feed him without disturbing a sleeping dad.

It would be especially tempting for bottle-feeding mums to take advantage of dad in the night. Some bottle-feeding mums allow dad to give baby the late evening feed, so that they can go to bed early and get some rest, and then take over again in the night. This works well for those night-owl dads.

Of course there are always exceptions, and illness would be one. If you or baby are sick or just going through a particularly unsettled period, then dad will probably be willing to help out during the night shift. Especially if that is the exception rather than the rule!

# Chapter Twelve

# Playtime
## What to do when
## They are Awake

After spending much of our time feeding, settling, and watching our babies sleep, it is fun to spend some quality time awake with them.

But what do we do with them?

In this chapter, we will look at some playtime activities:

> **How Long will he Stay Awake?**
>
> **Three Phases of Awaketime**
>
> **Mozart and Dance Lessons**

## How Long will he Stay Awake?

*Realistic Awaketimes*

New little babies do not need much awaketime.

They tire easily (especially if they were born a little early), and a tired baby doesn't feed well or sleep well. This may mean that a problem which looks to be a problem with feeding or sleeping can actually be a problem with a baby being over-stimulated by being kept up for too long.

Up until 3 months of age, a baby need not routinely be awake (from the time he has woken for a feed) for longer than 45-60 minutes. If he is feeding roughly 3 hourly or less, than 45 minutes is plenty. If he is going a little longer between feeds (up to around 4 hours), then 60 minutes is usually plenty. Trying to keep a newborn up regularly for 1½ hours or more is only going to create problems with his sleeping.

Some mums are encouraged to look for tired signs before putting baby to bed. This can be helpful – if you see tired signs, then definitely put baby to bed. But don't necessarily wait for signs before putting him to bed every time. Some babies just don't show tired signs until they are well and truly overtired. And once he is overtired, he will struggle to get to sleep and to stay asleep.

Between 3 and 6 months, a baby's awaketime will gradually stretch from around 1 hour to around 2 hours (followed by around 2 hours of sleep).

> **Once he is overtired, he will struggle to get to sleep and to stay asleep.**

Between 6 and 12 months, your baby may have one or two periods of around 2–2½ hours of awaketime (often in the morning and after lunch), and one slightly longer stretch of around 3-3½ hours awaketime (often in the late afternoon).

### *Stretching and Cutting Back*

If baby's awaketimes have just been too long and he needs to go to bed earlier, then it is just a matter of wrapping him up and putting him to bed. He may not be happy about it so a little perseverance with his protestations may be required, possibly followed by some sleep training.

If baby has been put to bed too early, then he may keep waking early for feeds. This makes it difficult to stretch out those feed times. Try to keep him awake a little longer after a feed by talking, singing, playing with him or even using wet washers to wash his face. Nappy changes, and even bathing can help keep him awake for that extra 5-10 minutes or so.

### *Outings*

Timing short outings for awaketime is ideal. If he doesn't sleep while out, and ends up being awake for longer than normal, you can try cuddling him or using a sling to see if he'll sleep. Or maybe walk him in his pram. If he still refuses, then try allowing slightly shorter awaketimes through the rest of the day back at home to catch up.

## Three Phases of Awaketime

As baby gets older, it is very helpful to divide up parts of his awaketime into three main areas: **time with mum, time near mum** and **time alone.**

Of course a newborn isn't going to benefit much from this. But as he gets bigger he will enjoy these different phases of his awaketime.

These different times might only last a few minutes each when he is little. Gradually, those times will lengthen. The phases won't necessarily be the same length of time either – some may be only a few minutes, and others will be longer. Some days it may not happen at all.

### Time *With Mum*

This is a precious time of cuddles, reading and singing with mum. Or of course dad, siblings, and other relatives and friends.

It is handy to finish baby's awaketime with this one. It can also be helpful if you are stretching a awaketime a little or if baby needs a little settling or calming before bedtime.

### Time *Near Mum*

This involves playing with toys while watching mum (or dad) from a short distance in the rocker chair or bouncer, while she is working in the kitchen or pottering around.

Baby may be looking quietly around the room or perhaps even jumping in a Jolly Jumper.

As he gets bigger, he can sit in a high chair while watching the action in the kitchen or sit in a pram while the washing is going out on the line. He can play on a mat with a basket of toys or on the grass while mum is gardening.

All of these activities are things he is doing on his own, but still with some interaction from mum.

### Time Alone

This is a time to give him some playtime alone, and without constant interaction with mum.

Even a newborn can have a few minutes on the floor by himself. This will give him an opportunity to stretch and kick his legs and arms, and allow any trapped wind to escape. He might also enjoy sitting up and watching the family in a rocker chair, with a rattle or mobile. As he gets older, time in a sturdy high chair or mat play whilst you are watching from a distance can be play alone time.

Using a playpen for a short time twice a day (morning and afternoon) can also be a part of this phase of awaketime. For younger babies, just a few minutes are plenty. This time will gradually increase as they get older. More on playpens later.

## Mozart and Dance Lessons

### Over-stimulation

If a young baby is over-stimulated during his awaketime, he may find it difficult to get back to sleep. Or may wake during sleeps unable to resettle.

**Over-stimulation is a very common cause of unsettledness and night waking in young babies.**

He is less likely to become over-stimulated if his awaketime is fairly calm when he is little. It isn't always possible to keep him calm - especially if there are visitors, outings or siblings. So if he has been somewhat over-stimulated, don't be surprised if he becomes a little grumpy. It can't always be avoided and is often just part of life.

Over-stimulation is a very common cause of unsettledness and night waking in young babies. It is worth keeping those awaketimes to appropriate lengths!

Listening to Mozart might be a fun thing to do with a newborn. *Dancing* to Mozart is probably over-doing it until he is a little bigger!

### The Wall Observer

Many parents worry that their new baby is more interested in the wall than mum's face. Perhaps they can't see? Or maybe there is something wrong? No, they are usually quite normal. They are just checking out that great big space around them. Perhaps they have already spent time focussing on faces, and need to rest their eyes. Some babies are chronic wall observers, and others are face observers. Both are normal.

If as time goes on, your baby does not seem to grow out of this stage, then have him checked out to put your mind at rest.

### Baby Games

Babies are fairly simple, and so simple games are fine and come naturally to most parents.

He has nothing to compare you to, so don't be afraid to behave in a silly way to get him to smile

> He can't understand everything you say, but he will enjoy listening to the rhythms in your voice.

or pay attention to you! Singing, silly faces and noises, simple books, interesting toys, pets, and different textures will all fill up his awaketime in these first few months.

Chat to him as you go about doing things. While he can't understand everything you say, he will enjoy listening to the rhythms in your voice. Listening to mum's speech helps later with language development.

### *Music and Massage*

Listening to music with your baby is fun.

There are whole industries trying to give babies a start in their intellectual lives by encouraging them listen to various types of classical music. This is fun, but not essential.

Some parents even go overboard and fill their baby's awaketime with many stimulating activities in order to give them a head start in life. Like popping them in front of very large TV screens to watch swirly patterns while listening to music. For hours! Or dancing around and around the room to music every day.

But babies do not need TV, dance lessons and music appreciation classes in these first couple of months. Save that for down the track.

Massage is another industry that has targeted mothers and their new babies. While massage is relaxing and comforting (for mum as much as baby), it is not necessary for baby to sleep well. By all means use massage as part of a awaketime activity if you wish. But again, too much of a good thing can sometimes backfire so that both mum and baby become over-dependent on massage in order to settle.

### *Stay Outta my Face!*

Some new mums just adore their first babies so much, that they cannot resist the urge to **be there** every moment of baby's awaketime.

So much so, that baby doesn't get a chance to look at anyone or anything else. Ever. Let alone have cuddles with friends and relatives.

If you feel yourself drawn to your baby's every glance, then it may take some effort to back off a little. Give him an opportunity to observe and enjoy other people and other views of the world every now and again.

*Cousins, Siblings and Friends*

A new mother is very (understandably) protective.

Our new first babies seem so precious and fragile that surely an enthusiastic young visitor will break them somehow! But babies are tough little things, and can cope with a surprising amount of poking, picking up, carrying around, and loud overtures from other little people. Watch, without hovering too much, and allow your baby to be part of the world of other little people. He will be fine (most of the time!).

> **A new mother is very (understandably) protective.**

On the other hand, totally unsupervised playtime between babies and toddlers is not wise. If an older sibling or cousin is prone to being a little too rough, then much closer supervision is going to be needed. Perhaps you could use this time as training time in gentleness for that bigger child.

*Playpens: Joy or Jail?*

For an adult, the thought of being stuck in the confines of a playpen can seem like a jail sentence! But babies are only little and have a different view of their world.

Playpens as part of a routine, are very handy tools that can help little ones to have some focused play. It is ideal to start at around 4 months or so. Or even earlier for self-protection if there are older siblings!

After breakfast and again in the afternoon after feeding is good for playpen time. Baby is then well fed and well rested and much more likely to enjoy this time playing alone.

Some babies are content to play happily in a playpen that is in the living room (like my little Rosie), with household activity not disturbing them at all. While others need to be isolated a little more from the hustle and bustle of family life (like my young Elliot). Perhaps in the corner of a bedroom or study.

A mobile or a few toys are usually all you need - depending on the age of the baby. Few toys are better than too many which can be overwhelming to a little one.

Start with 5 minutes and cheerfully pull him out at the end (regardless of how happy or unhappy he is), and then gradually extend the time. Sometimes a music tape is helpful. Baby learns that when that final song comes on, it's pack up time.

It is possible for a baby to happily spend up to an hour in the playpen by the time he is around 9-10 months old. Use this opportunity to teach him to pack up by cheerfully packing up his toys, and encouraging him to help. He will start getting the idea when he is a little bit bigger.

# Chapter Thirteen

# When One Becomes Two

The thought of adding another little one to a family can be exciting – or scary! Many parents wonder if they'll ever love another child as much as the first. Thankfully, God allows our love to be multiplied rather than divided with more children, and it is a rare family that regrets the arrival of another blessing.

There are some things to think through when imagining how it will all work with another baby, plus a toddler in the house. Many parents worry about how it will all work out.

In this chapter we will briefly discuss some of the main areas of concern for parents, and some extra tips that we learned along the way.

While a new baby is a little bewildering to a toddler, he will soon get used to the idea and forget those carefree days of being an only child. I had a little chat with a young 3 year old recently about his new baby brother. He looked up at me with solemn eyes and said, "Daddy's bringing it home today." He sounded so unexcited! I really don't think we need to psychoanalyse our little ones. A new baby is mysterious, but he'll get used to it.

So how do we juggle with more than one? Let's look at some of those common areas of concern.

### Breastfeeding with a Toddler in Tow

The majority of mums will go on to have a second baby while the first little one is still a toddler.

So how do we manage to breastfeed with an audience?

> **Please don't feel guilty if you find yourself watching Bananas in Pyjamas while feeding!**

One of the helpful things about having a flexible routine in your day is that you are be able to plan your days with both feeding baby and managing toddler in mind.

My first baby Madeline was 19 months old when little Oliver was born. The next few babies came with a similar gap. So feeding with a curious toddler (or several) looking on became the norm in our house!

A very helpful start to the day was to feed the baby before the toddler was up and about. This meant that baby was often ready to go back to bed at breakfast time, and toddler and I could get on with our day. Likewise, my toddlers were usually asleep during the afternoon baby feed, so it was a fairly peaceful time with baby.

It's that middle morning feed that becomes the highlight of toddler's day. In those first few weeks when you may be extra tired and overwhelmed, please don't feel guilty if you find yourself watching Bananas in Pyjamas while feeding! This is just a season, and a few weeks of videos is just part of this stage of life. It will keep that curious, mischievous toddler in sight and happily occupied so that you can concentrate on giving your baby a good feed. As baby gets bigger and you feel more able, you can use this time for reading books with your toddler, watching him do puzzles, playing in the yard or other activities that don't involve watching videos.

The other feed to juggle with toddler is usually the late afternoon feed. Again those Bananas may come to help, or perhaps Dad may be home to help keep an eye on your little adventurer. It is a juggle, but you can do this! Plan your toddler's day with feeds in mind to reduce the risk of chaos.

*Juggling Capsules and School-runs*

As your babies grow in size and multiply in number, you will no doubt end up trying to juggle school and preschool trips with a new baby at some point.

With your first baby, you could plan all your outings around baby's feeds. But with older siblings, it becomes the other way around. And if your school trips are long, it can become tricky.

You can try feeding baby in the car while waiting for school to finish. Or feed baby first then go straight out. Or pluck a sleeping baby out of bed, into the car, and then back to bed again at the end of the trip. You will no doubt end up planning your baby's routine with these school trips in mind.

Have confidence that these younger siblings are remarkably versatile, and much more adaptable than our first babies. Some juggling and experimenting may be needed, but they will probably stress over interruptions less than us mums!

*Baby Two and Routine*

Just like Baby One thrived on flexible routine, so will Baby Two (and beyond). All babies are a little different however, so you will find yourself making a few subtle changes to adapt to a different personality.

**These younger siblings are remarkably versatile!**

My number one baby Madeline was like many first babies. She preferred things to be quiet and consistent, and didn't like sudden changes in her day. Little Oliver, who arrived 19 months after Madeline, was so relaxed! He coped so well with changes and a busy household. We learned to accommodate him quite easily because he was so easy-going.

You may find the same, or you may discover that it works out the other way around. Perhaps your first was easy-going, but your second is more highly strung. Don't panic – all is normal, and you will learn to adapt to his personality as you did with your first. There should be no need to throw everything out the window – just a tweak here and there to help this different personality fit into the family.

### Feeding Differences

Just like there may be some small variations in routine, there will also be some differences in the way babies feed. Perhaps Baby One didn't breastfeed very well (or at all), and this next one takes to it like a house on fire. Madeline was a beautiful baby but rather stubborn to breastfeed. Oliver attached like a vacuum cleaner and fed like a pro! Things were so much easier the second time around.

However it might work the other way around in your house. This could be rather frustrating for you if Baby One was a great feeder but Baby Two is not. Persevere if you can but in the end you can only do your best ☺.

### Crying

Babies all cry differently.

Madeline went straight to full blast every time. Oliver started and stopped, and never really got too worked up. Rosie never cried at all, and Elliot protested everything! We just need to get used to our new baby's way of crying and learn to adapt, without expecting that this one will behave the same as the first.

If your new baby's cry is alarming in it's tone (persistent, or even weak), then it is certainly wise to have him checked out.

### Sharing Rooms

> **Our children have always shared a room with someone.**

Should we put our new baby in with our first baby?

Our children have always shared a room with someone. Six children in a three bedroom house can get squishy and we are all quite used to living with other people!

We found that putting a newborn to sleep in a room with an older sibling is rather disruptive during the night, so our little ones have slept in a portable basket that can be easily moved about the house. They have been fine to room in with older siblings once they are sleeping through the night.

Most older siblings adapt rather quickly to unusual night disruptions. Wet beds, vomiting, nightmares, falling out of bed – it all happens with children at sometime, and makes it no reason to panic about having few bedrooms. Our older siblings may or may not wake up (usually they don't), but after reassurance, always go back to sleep again.

Of course, it is wonderful if you do have a spare bedroom for a new baby. Perhaps you could shuffle Baby Two into Baby One's room, on Baby Three's arrival ☺.

### Cot to Bed

When to move a baby from cot to bed?

In our house it was when the next one needed the cot! For us, that meant around two years or so. Babies can move earlier or later than that if needed.

There will be some training needed. A toddler in a big bed will need some time to adjust, so some patience and consistency with training will be needed for a little while until he does. Our special rule for toddlers was "feet stay on the bed!" We used a bed guard as a visual reminder that they were supposed to stay in bed and as a safeguard in case they fell out in the night.

If your babies are quite close together (a year or so), you may consider buying a second cot.

### Afternoon Sleeps (for mum!)

When there was only one baby, a quiet afternoon nap was a distinct possibility. But now – it looks much more impractical!

> **It is conceivable to plan your feeds and naps so you can have at least one quiet hour in the day.**

It is conceivable to plan your feeds and naps so you can have at least one quiet hour in the day. It may mean rearranging your toddler's naps so that he goes down a little earlier or later, and you can have a quick snooze before baby's next feed. And it will be worth it – a new baby is tiring enough but even more so without a break from your rather active toddler!

### Expectations versus Reality

With one baby, it was just about possible to maintain your tidy house and keep up with all those things you have loved to do.

But with another baby in the house, don't be surprised if you feel a little frayed around the edges. I have always noticed that with one baby we can keep a foot in the door of our old life. But with two it becomes rather stressful. And with three? Just about impossible. I can't believe the things I tried to keep up with when I had two or three little ones!

The reality is that with a baby plus a toddler, you are not going to be able to keep up with everything. The house will look a little more lived in (toys to trip over, clean washing to be put away). The meals will be a little more basic (sausages sound gourmet). You won't spend 40 minutes getting yourself ready to go out (as long as you and the children are dressed – you are ready). An evening out will be the last thing you want (I'd rather just have an early night).

This is normal. Letting go of our old lives and embracing our new life – Motherhood – is part of growing up. There is no need to feel guilty or that we need to live up to that seemingly perfect supermum down the road (or on TV)!

> **Letting go of our old lives and embracing our new life – Motherhood – is part of growing up.**

### Toddler Activities

It will be very tempting to sign up for all those essential toddler activities. Music Appreciation lessons. Swimming lessons. Gymbaroo. Playgroup. Ballet. Early Reading lessons.

But running your toddler (and consequently baby) around to all these activities will lead to your own exhaustion, a grumpy and over-tired toddler, and a baby who just won't settle.

While good in themselves, all these activities are not necessary for every toddler. Slow down and spend this time playing with him. Perhaps one or two activities in a week are plenty. Your baby will sleep better, and your toddler is just as happy with your company ☺.

### Toddler Troubles

Most mums have few problems with their new second baby, especially in comparison to that tricky toddler!

If you are finding that your toddler is giving you trouble, you are not alone. A new baby will mean a period of adjustment for your toddler, and his anxiety at the change in routine will likely come out in some unusual behaviours for a short time. Food issues, sleep issues, bath issues, separation issues – these are not abnormal. With some patient and consistent understanding and training from mum and dad, he will most likely settle down in time and once again be a joy to be around.

Adding new babies to a house is such an exciting time. It is busy too, and you will soon wonder how you spent your time when you only had one ☺.

> **Adding new babies to a house is such an exciting time!**

Relax, slow down, and enjoy those first few weeks and months with more little people. Try not to do too many things – many mums feel that they need to keep up a ferocious pace. These days pass quickly and it may not be long until the pitter-pattering of little feet return yet again ☺.

### *When they keep coming (and coming…)*

Some folks find themselves outnumbered by little people. Having three or four little ones under school-age is about the busiest, most overwhelming time of life! I had four under five (and eventually six under nine) and I can remember feeling like I was living in a bit of a fog most days. Where to start?

Some people like to have their whole day ordered. Other people can live with more of a go-with-the-flow approach to life.

But unless you want to spend your whole day chasing your tail and putting out fires, you will need to organise you and your busy household into some sort of routine.

I found it helpful to start with baby. Having a basic plan for managing your baby's feeds and sleeps will help you plan for your toddler's day. Then work up from the next youngest. Plan (on paper) sleeps, meals, and playtime. Try to keep everyone busy with something – so that there are few (if any) times that one of these little ones is left wandering around doing 'nothing'. Plan their playtime activities so that you are not left chasing after what they might decide to do at any moment. Rather, you can anticipate their needs and activities, and remain **pro-active** in your parenting rather than re-active.

Enforce rest times. You need some space for an hour or two to prepare for the afternoon and evening busyness, and they need time to have a rest too, even if they are too old to sleep. Books on bed for an hour might be just the thing!

Give them regular, age-appropriate chores to do everyday. These start very simple (putting shoes away), and as they get older, become more complex (unpacking the dishwasher or sweeping the floor). This not only helps the family (and some days it won't feel helpful at all), but it trains them to pitch in and be part of a little community.

Nurture your marriage. Working as a team will help those days flow more smoothly. And it is good to know that you have the support of your husband. Spend a few minutes each day (breakfast or after dinner) catching up with him while the kids are around to see so that they can be reminded that you are friends. If we save all our chat times until they are in bed, they won't be able to observe our friendship. Have an occasional night out with him alone to recharge without the chatter of toddlers. Ask him for his thoughts on particular issues with the children, so that he is included in what is happening throughout the day with them.

Try to be consistent with managing your children. When there are a few of them and they are each at different ages and stages, it is easy to lose track of who is who and what you are doing with each of them. I found that writing a list of who was doing what helped on those foggy days. I would stick my list on the fridge - with feeding and sleeping times, activities etc on display to remind myself of what I was doing.

Spend some time each day just enjoying them! We can get so focused on getting through each busy day that we forget to enjoy them, play with them, read to them, and do fun spontaneous things with them.

While being a very busy time it is also a precious time of stories, cuddles, chatter and learning. And believe it or not, it does go very quickly ☺.

# Chapter Fourteen

# Twins,
# Premmies
# and Special Babies

Sometimes we get more than we bargained for!

If your baby becomes two babies, or arrives a little (or a lot) earlier than expected, or your baby is born with some special needs that require some special management, you may end up wondering if it will mean a drastic change in how you manage your baby. Can you still use a flexible routine? Perhaps you have used a flexible routine with your first baby, and are wondering how you might do things differently this time around to accommodate your baby's special needs.

I am not personally experienced in the areas of twins, premmies and special needs babies.

However I have dear friends who have experienced something unexpected with their babies and they have been kind enough to share a few brief tips with us, in case you have a little surprise (or two!) in your house.

Of course none of these tips should be taken as medical advice – please see your doctor for that. These are just mum-to-mum tips from those who have been there...

## Twins (by mum Kerrie)

*What are some feeding tips for twins?*
If breastfeeding (which is often very possible with twins), allocate each baby their own breast, feeding them from this breast at every feed. This allows each baby to demand the

supply they need. When feeding, feed them from their own side then burp them, and put them back on that same side again. If the heaviest baby is on the right breast (or left, if you are left handed), it will be easier to burp them.

Keep both babies on the same sleep/wake routine. This may mean waking one or both babies to feed them together.

You will need to feed your babies in a football hold – which is easier than it sounds. In those first few days or weeks when the babies are just getting used to learning to feed, nurse them one after the other. Once you get the hang of it you are ready to try simultaneous feeding.

> **Keep both babies on the same sleep / wake routine.**

Attach one baby using a football hold on your left breast (if you are right handed), and use a rolled up cloth nappy to 'chock' behind the baby to keep him in place. This will free up your hands to position the other baby on the right breast. If you 'chock' this baby also, your hands will be free to keep the babies awake or to burp them.

A twin feeding pillow will also make it easier to feed the babies simultaneously. These are large and cumbersome to carry about but make feeding much easier, and they are sizable enough to last until your babies are quite big. They can be bought from various places, including The Foam Booth, in Surry Hills, Sydney.

When the time comes to wean your babies, take your time to drop each of the feeds if possible. Drop one feed (eg lunch time), then wait up to two weeks before dropping the next feed, and so on. Because you are producing double the amount of milk compared to most mums, it is best to drop feeds gradually to allow your supply to adjust. Otherwise you could end up feeling engorged for a while, or you could even develop mastitis.

Perhaps you are bottle-feeding your twins and want to feed them at the same time. If you don't have a helper to share the feeding with then you may consider feeding your twins in their double pram. This way you can hold their bottles at the same time. Just make sure you give each of them a lovely long cuddle afterwards.

*What are some tips for awaketime with twins?*

Try to occasionally stagger awaketime activities throughout the day so that you get to spend one-on-one time with each baby. For example, you might sit and read books with one baby on your lap while the other baby has some tummy time on the mat, or is in the playpen.

Two portable cots are essential. As well as providing a portable place for your babies to sleep, they also double as playpens. When your babies are old enough for playpen time, you will have the option of putting them into their own playpens for simultaneous playpen time. This will allow you some time to yourself or time to tidy the house!

It's also handy (although not essential) to have two baby seats/ bouncers. As well as being useful for awaketime, these can double as portable high-chairs when you are out visiting friends.

*What are some tips for sleeptime with twins?*

You can put both babies to sleep in the same cot until they are around 3 months of age. After that age they tend to start rolling around, or they grow tall enough to bump heads! Tuck each baby down towards each end of the cot.

One crying baby will not wake the other if you keep them in the same room from the beginning.

*Overall, how did you apply the idea of routine with your twins?*

My twins had the same flexible routine as a single baby would. I kept both babies on the same feed-wake-sleep routine from the start. For example, in the early days my son usually woke earlier than my daughter during the night, so I would wake my daughter and feed her at the same time.

*Any encouraging tips?*

Twins are definitely a double blessing. They are twice the love, without twice the work (except for the washing)!

*Anything particular to watch out for?*

Keep an eye on your babies' growth charts to make sure they are growing well and getting plenty of milk.

Don't worry about one baby waking the other. If you give them the chance, your twins can easily get used to blocking out noises such as the other baby crying. The result can be a couple of really great sleepers!

*Thank-you to Kerrie Noakes, mum of three, including twins Joel and Phoebe, for sharing her twins tips.*

## Premmie Babies (by mum Natalie)

*What are some feeding tips for premmies?*

Your premmie will no doubt spend some time in hospital following his birth. This could be a few extra days, weeks or even months, depending on how early he is born and whether there are any other health issues to be managed.

However it is possible to achieve breastfeeding, even if it will take some time before baby is big enough to attach properly. It is also possible, depending on the prematurity of the baby, that baby will need to be fed with a feeding tube for some time. During this time make sure that

> **It is possible to achieve breastfeeding- even if it will take some time before baby is big enough to attach properly.**

you pump during the day at regular 4 hourly intervals. This will allow some of your milk to be saved and given to baby via bottle or feeding tube, and will also give stimulation to your breasts so that you will be able to attempt to breastfeed down the track.

Avoid pumping through the night. You need to be well rested to have enough energy to deal with hospital visits and the emotional roller-coaster of having a very tiny baby. Day pumping is sufficient for now.

Hospital staff are very familiar with the needs of premmie babies, so follow their advice without getting too stressed about your breastfeeding. Just getting through each day will be stressful enough.

Once baby comes home, you can pick up with feeding on a 3-4 hour routine (depending on the age and size of your baby). Most neo-natal wards in hospitals are feeding babies on a routine so you may only need to continue the routine with which your baby is already familiar.

Be patient and take care not to attempt to over-feed your baby. If he drinks too much some issues could arise. His immature digestive system, his possibly immature lungs, or excessive coughing, may cause him to vomit his feed back up. If he does struggle with underdeveloped lungs, he may struggle a little to breathe and suck at the same time – even from a bottle.

> **Your baby will gain weight at quite a different rate to that of a full-term baby.**

Be comfortable with your baby's regular, consistent weight gain rather than comparing him to a full-term baby. Your baby will gain weight at quite a different rate to that of a full-term baby.

*What are some sleeping and awaketime tips for a premmie?*

While your premmie is in hospital he will have almost no awaketime. Premmie babies gain weight while they are sleeping and too much stimulation will have more serious consequences for their growth.

Enjoy the time with him while he is awake (brief though it may be), and enjoy watching him sleep (which is most of the time). Unlike a full term baby, a little premmie will often fall asleep in your arms. This is fine – when he needs to go to sleep he will!

Once you bring your baby home it is most helpful to continue to follow the routine that he has been on in hospital. Take care that your premmie will likely have a much shorter awaketime than a full-term baby to begin with. Once your baby is bigger, his awaketimes will increase so that he eventually catches up to a normal baby of his age.

Some premmies will come home on monitors and oxygen. Try not to get too stressed with having to manage all this equipment, and with sounds of alarms going off. Try to 'go with the flow' and enjoy your baby as much as you can. Remember that these special considerations are not permanent – but temporary until your baby is bigger.

*Overall, how did you apply the idea of routine with your premmie?*

Once your baby is home, he will follow a flexible routine just like a full-term baby. You may just need to make some adjustments and keep a close eye on his weight gain to make sure he is getting the feeds and sleeps that he needs to grow.

Remember that he will be a little 'younger' in his age for some weeks or even months, depending on his prematurity. For those very tiniest of babies, it may take several years for him to physically catch up with his peers. He may even have other challenges as a result of his early birth that you are also managing. Surgeries, therapy and on-going special needs may add to the mix of things to juggle.

Start him on a newborn routine from the time he comes home from hospital, despite his actual age. Once his feeding patterns of 3-4 hours have been established and all is going well, he will gradually stretch out his routine until he has caught up again. This may take days, weeks or months.

*Any encouraging tips?*

As much as possible, try to treat your baby as a normal baby – without fussing over him.

*Anything particular to watch out for?*

It can become easy with a premmie baby that has had special care from birth, to over-compensate and be a little too lax and flexible with his routine. If you become way too flexible because you have had a rough ride with him early on, you may find that things start to unravel. Better to stay on track.

Watch also that if you have other children, you spend special time with them too. Because they are also special ☺.

*Special thanks to Natalie Dixon for her insights into managing a premmie baby. Mum of four, including Lazarus, born at 25 weeks.*

## Special Needs Babies (by mums Louise and Megan)

*What are some feeding tips for Special Needs Babies?*

Special Needs Babies cover a large range of babies – babies who are ill, or who are born with physical deformities (ranging from those which can be corrected with surgery, to those which will affect them for life), or who have an intellectual disability, or those with a combination of these. For some of these babies their special needs are temporary, while for others they are permanent and ongoing. Some of these tips may be applicable to some babies and not to others. Other tips will be applicable to all babies with a special need.

If your baby is born with a special need, he may find breastfeeding difficult due to poor muscle tone or facial injury. You will need to pump regularly throughout the day to maintain your milk supply and provide a good source of nutrition for your baby. Night pumping is not usually necessary – it may only exhaust you further.

**Surround yourself with supportive people.**

Persevere with (day) pumping and with teaching your baby to breastfeed as long as you are able. Many babies with conditions that causes poor muscle tone, like Down Syndrome, can learn to suck. As their strength increases they may be able to breastfeed on a full term basis. Breastfeeding will in turn help to develop stronger muscle tone around the mouth and jaw, and will facilitate speech development later. Be patient though – it may take much time and perseverance on your part. Surround yourself with supportive people – your local baby health sister, your family and friends.

You may need to rely on a naso-gastric tube to feed followed by a bottle of expressed breast milk when starting out, until he is strong enough to take more bottles/breastfeeds. When starting out with breastfeeding, try 5 minutes each side, alternating several times to keep him stimulated enough to nurse. Wet washers on his feet, and keeping him unwrapped will also help him stay awake for those feeds.

Other babies, due to their particular issue just won't be able to breastfeed. You can still pump milk for as long as you are able, so that he can have the best food from you. In the end it is more important that he gains

> **A feeding routine that is established early brings comfort and expectation to a baby.**

weight and grows. So do what you need to do to help that happen. Consider medical advice where necessary – a baby with serious health issues (eg looming heart operation) may need to gain weight faster than they can while struggling to breastfeed with poor muscle tone, and so bottle or tube feeding may be recommended.

Your special baby may be unusually sleepy, or unable to communicate their hunger with crying, so it will be important to wake him to feed on a regular routine in order for him gain weight at a healthy rate. A special needs baby, especially one on a bottle, may stretch those feed times out earlier so that they are truly hungry at feedtime, and more able to stay awake for a full feed.

With special needs children, communication can often be a barrier particularly in the early years. A feeding routine that is established early brings comfort and expectation to a baby as their body learns the difference between the sensations of being "full" as opposed to being "hungry". The discomfort of being hungry causes the baby to (usually) cry, which in turn gathers a response from mum. Baby feels hungry, mum responds by feeding, baby is full and happy. Baby learns to expect the next feed at the routine time, and responds (communicates) accordingly.

When introducing solids, seek advice from other mums and the clinic sister for when and what types may be best for your baby. While having a close and supportive extended family is wonderful, balancing their inexperienced advice on feeding your baby with that of a more experienced clinic sister may avoid some unhealthy eating habits starting too early.

*What are some awaketime tips for a special needs baby?*

Your special baby will probably have similar awaketimes to a regular baby, especially once that sleepy newborn period has passed. If you are spending parts of, or much of his week travelling to doctor appointments, you may find his awaketime is longer than you might like, or that he needs to catch sleep when he can. You will need to be flexible and stay on track when you can.

If your baby has poor muscle tone, he may have less than average neck strength and require plenty of tummy time to strengthen those muscles further. You may find as he gets bigger and can enjoy longer awaketimes, that you are striving towards various physical goals with your special baby. These awaketimes will be times of exercising his muscles and encouraging him to build up his strength.

Your baby may also be calmed by some quiet and gentle classical music during parts of his awaketime, especially close to sleeptime.

*What are some sleeping tips for a special needs baby?*

Your special needs baby may be more sleepy than other babies. This will mean that it will be important to wake him for feeds (so that he will gain weight). If you are out and about frequently with medical appointments and such, you may need to be more flexible with his sleep times so that he gets all the sleep that he needs despite the interruptions to his routine.

Try not to let 5 hours pass between feedings during the day. Nights can go longer – and indeed it may be better to allow baby to sleep as long as he wishes during the night. Better (as long as your doctor is happy) for mum to have that time of rest during the night too! If you do need to add an expressing session in the night for your own milk supply, than that is fine. You can give it to baby during the day if you need to.

Keep that pattern of feed/wake/sleep as best as possible, despite your sleepy baby. It takes a lot of energy to feed and he does need lots of sleep. And keep him tightly wrapped for his sleeps too. The wrap will help stop him from scratching his face and waking himself up.

*Overall, how did you apply the idea of routine with your special needs baby?*

Applying a flexible routine is not difficult at all. With a sleepy baby it is more of an effort to wake him for feeds than teaching him to resettle himself in order to fit into a routine. That predictable, flexible routine enables you to be sure that he is getting all the feeds that he needs to grow, and opportunities for sleep as well. When the days are hectic with appointments and such, having that routine helps you to stay on track. The consistent and predictable routine also allows the rest of the family to run smoothly while baby settles in. And it allows mum to get some much needed rest so that she can have more energy to manage the family.

*Any encouraging tips?*

Be sure to talk with other parents who have similar issues with their babies. They will have tips and encouragement for you and you can support each other. Read and learn all about your baby's special needs so that you can know what to expect with him during this first year.

Have a 'Renew Your Spirit Day' and a 'Family Fun Day' now and again. Take baby steps with the cleaning and laundry. Build up routines gradually for all family members, to take on morning chores, and have an evening routine to prepare for the following day.

Smile more, laugh at yourself, encourage and hug your husband in the evening and do something for yourself everyday ☺. If you have a rough day, just tick it off and start again tomorrow.

While routines are great, try not to bury yourself in it. Be flexible with managing doctor/specialist appointments and visiting with friends.

*Anything particular to watch out for?*

Your special baby may well need surgery, therapy, and multiple doctor visits. This is going to mean a busy time for your family as you travel and accommodate a busy schedule around baby. There may also be much more stress and worry than with a baby without special needs, as you manage his illness or requirements. You will probably learn to 'go with the flow', and balance your busy moments with those quiet family moments.

Watch out for "bending the rules" too much though, just because your baby is extra special. If you set yourself a goal and some guidelines on how to get there, then stick with it – it will be worth the effort!

If you are using a fairly predictable routine, you can plan for naps of your own, or times of popping out to the shops or visiting - knowing when baby will be waking ready for the next feed.

Routines are great because they give mum, dad, baby, and the rest of the family some predictability about the structure to their day that provides comfort to everyone.

*Special thanks to Louise Lavilles for sharing her experiences with a special needs baby. Mum of five, including Nathaniel, with Down Syndrome*

*Special thanks also to Megan Collins, mum to three little girls, including Grace, with Down Syndrome.*

# Chapter Fifteen

# Dads
## A Brief Word

Congratulations on becoming a Dad!

Dads are very important.

There is no need for a new dad to be relegated to a position of unimportance or irrelevance. While you may not be the one to actually feed the baby, you will be the rock that keeps each day flowing smoothly in those first few weeks.

Most new dads these days are able to take a week or two off work to give them time to adjust to their new life of Fatherhood. This is wonderful! Once you go back to work however, your support is just as important to Mum. Just as Mum's life has changed forever, so too has Dad's.

You have two main roles in those first few months: caring for Mum (being a husband), and caring for Baby (being a dad).

## Caring For Mum

Mum will need a good few weeks to fully recover from giving birth.

**Assemble the pram. Cook her dinner. Share some chocolate...**

She will most likely be physically exhausted. Giving birth is hard work, and then to have to feed a baby around the clock puts a strain on the body that cannot be fully anticipated. She may be sore from stitches or from a caesarean. She may be weak from the delivery. Carry that baby capsule for her. Assemble the pram. Cook her dinner. Share some chocolate...

Dads

She may on the other hand, tell you she feels fine after a week or two. But her body still needs to heal. She may be determined to rush around doing everything she likes to do and that is great. In this case, she may need to be reminded by you (the Dad) to slow down and take it easy for a little while longer.

Be helpful! Ask her how you can help. What can you do to make things easier for her? Hang out the washing? Clean up the kitchen? Change a dirty nappy or three?

As time goes on and she is feeling much more like herself physically, hopefully you will work out between you the best way you can continue to help and support her.

Please don't forget to be a husband. Before the arrival of baby you were a couple, a team. You talked together. You laughed together. You went for walks together. You ate together. You went out together.

You are still a couple! Take time each day to remind your wife that you love her as a woman and a wife and not just as a new mummy. Spend time listening to her talk about her day and talking over your own day with her. Go for walks together (with the baby in the pram), and take her out for dinner now and again. Bring baby along. Or leave baby with Grandma for an hour or two.

Spending time together as a couple is important not just for these first months, but for the many years of parenting to come. You will of course devote almost all your time at home to caring for your children in lots of different ways. But you also need to care for your wife. It seems a long way off now, but one day those children will grow up and leave and start their own lives. And you will want to remain best friends with your wife. Working on ways to nurture that friendship now will make it easier then.

Right now, as a new mum she is very focused on her job of caring for this new baby 24/7, and she will appreciate you treating her like the precious woman that she is to you.

Keep a close eye on how your wife is doing emotionally. Encourage her: "You are doing a GREAT job!" For most new mums feelings of uncertainty and fatigue are quite normal, but if you sense a real hopelessness is setting in and she is simply unable to shake those blues, take her along to her doctor to get some help. Post Natal Depression can happen to the best of mothers and symptoms needn't be ignored.

This book is divided into short chapters based on the different ages and stages of a young baby. I encourage you to read each section as your own baby approaches those ages, so that you can be aware of what your wife is trying to do with him. With you also having an idea of what is going on, you can keep a firm hand on the tiller to help provide a steady course for your wife. Especially on those days where she is struggling to see the bigger picture.

## Caring For Baby

Many new dads have never held a baby before, let alone changed nappies or bathed one. Hopefully you'll be an expert soon!

Some mums are equally inexperienced, and you will be learning together and sharing many of those responsibilities of caring for baby in those first weeks and months. While you may not be feeding baby, you can certainly have fun learning to burp baby after feeds. You can change nappies, play with baby, dress and bath baby. If your wife is unsure of herself, encourage her to take on some of those things so that she can manage when you are not there.

Some mums become a little possessive of their babies, and you may need to be patient or even encourage your wife to let you share some of the caring for your baby. If she continues to be reluctant to let you share some of those caring responsibilities, she may end up quite exhausted over time.

It is an awesome responsibility to raise a child. And there is much more to being a dad than changing nappies. As your baby

Dads

grows into a toddler and beyond, you will have countless opportunities to pass on your family's values and build character into your child.

Enjoy your child. Lead, teach, train and protect him. Be an example to him – for he is watching your every move! Look ahead to the next stage of the journey and prepare for it with wisdom and prayer.

*"Fathers, do not exasperate your children;*
*instead, bring them up in the training and instruction of the Lord."*
*Ephesians 6:4*

*"He who fears the Lord has a secure fortress,*
*and for his children, it will be a refuge." Proverbs 14:26*

# Chapter Sixteen

# A Final Word
# To Mum

Well here we are at the end of that first exciting year of Motherhood!

I pray that as your baby grows you will continue to enjoy him (or of course, her) as you have this first year.

The next few years bring their own challenges. Walking, talking, exploring, mischief. Spontaneous cuddles, messages of love, discovery and companionship.

And while this next year or two won't be quite as physically demanding as that first, it will still be draining at times. Especially if you welcome more little blessings into your home – and I hope you do ☺.

You have spent a good part of this first year establishing a healthy flexible routine for your baby, and I hope that you plan to continue with these good habits into the next few years with your toddler. Toddlers love routine! They just love the predictability of their days and knowing when things are going to happen.

So for sleeps, meals and playtime activities, a good routine will help those days flow more smoothly. You have no doubt heard of the "terrible twos", but I do believe that those twos don't need to be terrible at all. In fact those toddler years can be terrific!

Your little toddler will no doubt try to exert his will, and you will need to have a plan for managing his growing sense of independence. If you can plan ahead and be pro-active with him, you will reap rewards of peace and security in knowing the direction you are travelling together. From a calm and settled baby, you can have a calm and settled toddler. And you can remain a confident parent.

As a mum, I hope that you grow in the confidence that you are doing an amazing job! In a fast-paced world of business and materialism that often doesn't value mothers, remember that of all the women in the world, God chose YOU to be a mother to your child. And only you as his mother (and along with his father) can love your child, care for your child and prepare your child for the rest of his life in the way that is best for him. So take this job of yours seriously!

And as a wife, I pray that you will continue to nurture your marriage and value your husband as a partner to you in parenting, and as a father to your child. Love and cherish him, encourage and support him, and you will be, in turn, loved, encouraged and supported by him.

And at the end of the day, never forget the One who gave you this family. He who is the giver of all wisdom, and who will stand by you to the end. The Almighty God whose love never fails, but "always protects, always trusts, always hopes and always perseveres."

*"For I am convinced that neither death nor life, neither angels nor demons, neither the present nor the future, nor any powers, neither height nor depth, nor anything else in all creation, will be able to separate us from the love of God that is in Christ Jesus our Lord." Romans 8:38-39*

# Suggested Websites

**Babies:**

My Website: www.calmbabyconfidentmum.com

**Toddlers – The Next Step:**

Terrific Toddlers: www.terrifictoddlers.com.au

**Parenting:**

Growing Families Australia: www.gfi.org.au

4 The Family: 4thefamily.com.au

# Acknowledgements

Special thanks need to go my darling James and awesome children for their patience with me in the midst of book writing. And for the hours of help that James gave in formatting this book - thank you!

Thank-you also to those who have played a significant role in helping us shape the foundations of our parenting and family, and who have continuously taught, encouraged and supported us along the way. In particular, Gary and Anne-Marie Ezzo, Bill and Joan Grosser  and Leigh and Merrilyn Roberts.

Additionally, a thank-you to Kerrie, Natalie, Megan and Louise for their willingness to share some tips on managing their special babies, and to Penny, Kerrie and Alison for proof reading.

And finally much gratitude to Mel Hayde, for encouraging me to embark on this project, and for cheering me on ☺.